**DONALD
SCHMIDT**

**A FIVE SESSION
STUDY GUIDE**

Death of Jesus

FOR
Progressive
Christians

WOOD LAKE

Editor: Michael Schwartzentruber
Proofreader: Dianne Greenslade
Designer: Robert MacDonald

Library and Archives Canada Cataloguing in Publication
Title: Death of Jesus for progressive Christians.
Names: Schmidt, Donald, 1959- author.
Description: Written by Donald Schmidt. | "Bible study." | Includes
bibliographical references.
Identifiers: Canadiana (print) 20190197544 | Canadiana (ebook) 20190197552
| ISBN 9781773432793 (softcover) | ISBN 9781773432809 (HTML)
Subjects: LCSH: Passion narratives (Gospels) | LCSH: Jesus Christ–
Passion. | LCSH: Holy Week. | LCSH: Jesus Christ–Crucifixion.
Classification: LCC BT431.3 .S36 2019 | DDC 232.96–dc23

ISBN 978-1-77343-279-3

Published by Wood Lake Publishing Inc.
485 Beaver Lake Road, Kelowna, BC Canada V4V 1S5
www.woodlake.com | 250.766.2778

Wood Lake Publishing acknowledges the financial support of the
Government of Canada. Wood Lake also acknowledges the financial
support of the Province of British Columbia through the Book Publishing Tax
Credit.

Wood Lake Publishing acknowledges that we operate in the unceded
territory of the Syilx/Okanagan People, and we work to support
reconciliation and challenge the legacies of colonialism. The Syilx/Okanagan
territory is a diverse and beautiful landscape of deserts and lakes, alpine
forests and endangered grasslands. We honour the ancestral stewardship of
the Syilx/Okanagan People.

Printed in Canada. Printing 10 9 8 7 6 5 4 3 2 1

CONTENTS

6

Death of Jesus

FOR Progressive Christians

Dedicated to the late Marilyn Perry, friend and colleague for over 30 years, who frequently challenged me to enter into and become a part of the biblical story as a way of enhancing my faith journey;

and to Meg Jordan, friend and colleague for almost as long, who always challenged me to dig deeper, and never to feel like I understood the scriptures completely.

Thanks

Sincere gratitude to everyone at Wood Lake Publishing, who have an amazing desire to serve the progressive church, especially to Mike Schwartzentruber, editor extraordinaire, who helps an author see through their biases with humour, gentleness, and grace; to Robert MacDonald who designed the book and has made it user-friendly; and to Brian Thorpe and Jeannie Thompson for reading the manuscript and providing helpful suggestions.

For Group Study

On a recent trip to El Salvador I picked up a new Spanish translation of the Bible *(La Biblia de Nuestro Pueblo* or "The Bible of Our People"). On the back cover is a wonderful quotation from Saint Oscar Romero: "They are saying, then, that we do not read the Bible. Not only do we read the Bible but we analyze it, we celebrate it, we incarnate it, we want to make it our daily life" (11 November 1979).

The point of this study is to help you do just that: to analyze, celebrate, incarnate, and try to live out the powerful story of the events leading up to Jesus' death and burial.

This book is primarily designed to be used in a group setting, with minimal instruction for leadership. It is intended to encourage open conversation, for which this study guide is simply that – a guide. When your group gathers each week, you might want to spend a little time at the beginning compiling a list of thoughts, comments, and questions that have arisen for people during the week, pertaining to their readings about the events leading up to the death of Jesus. As a group, you can then try to address those during your conversation.

> **Did Jesus have to die?**
> **No.**
> **He didn't.**
> **He was killed.**
> **– Rob Bell,** *What Is the Bible?*

A good facilitator does *not* need to be a biblical scholar of any sort, just someone who can keep the session moving and the conversation on track. Leadership of the group could be held by one person or could change each time,

Death of Jesus
FOR Progressive Christians

but it is helpful to have a person in charge of the conversation so that the group does not get sidetracked or bogged down.

Spend time with the questions you'll find in the boxes scattered throughout the text; they are designed to provoke reflection. If your group is large – perhaps more than eight to ten people – you might want to divide into smaller groups to discuss the questions and to give people more time to share. But remember, whether you discuss the questions in the larger group or in smaller groups, there are no right or wrong answers. The goal is for group members to exchange thoughts, feelings, and opinions. The point is not to denigrate the stories we have, but rather to enhance our understanding of them. The exchange of ideas is key to achieving this outcome, which means it's okay for people to disagree. The facilitator should try to hold people's differences of opinion carefully, and help participants respect each other's views.

The facilitator will want to review each session ahead of time to get a sense of how much time to allot to the various questions and themes. The amount of time needed will depend on several factors, such as how many people are in the group, their familiarity with scripture, their theological stance, and so on.

For individual study

The best thing is simply to read the study along with a good translation of the Bible (preferably more than one so you can compare translations). Mark up the study guide with interesting things you learn from other sources, or with questions. Spend time pondering the questions that are listed. You might wish to write answers in the margins, but it's far more important to simply let the questions guide your thinking and reflection.

In writing this study, I kept a quotation in front of me. It comes from the beginning of Richard Attenborough's film *Gandhi:*

No man's life can be encompassed in one telling. There is no way to give each year its allotted weight, to include each event, each person who helped to shape a lifetime. What can be done is to be faithful in spirit to the record and try to find one's way to the heart of the man.

Accordingly, I have not included everything about the death of Jesus in this study – one simply cannot do that, without creating something quite unwieldy and clumsy. The passion story has been written about in hundreds if not thousands of books, and in many ways we have only scratched the surface. (One of the works used as a reference for this study contains almost 2,000 pages!) Thus, out of necessity, there are pieces I have left out. This may lead to questions I do not address, and I would refer you to any number of commentaries to explore issues of interest further (several good commentaries are listed on page 93).

Any study will, out of necessity, have to make arbitrary decisions about what to include. This one primarily includes the key gospel passages a person will hear on Palm/Passion Sunday – that is, the story of the triumphal entrance into Jerusalem and its immediate aftermath, and then the story of the Last Supper, and Jesus' subsequent arrest and "trials" up to and including his death and burial.

Of course, the resurrection of Jesus is the most important event for Christians, yet the events that led up to it are almost as important. To state the obvious, if Jesus had not died, the resurrection, regardless of how one

understands it, could not have happened. In the same way, the manner in which Jesus died is important. Had he died in a "normal" way, his death might not have taken on the significance it did. But he didn't die a "normal" death. According to all the biblical sources and a wide variety of non-biblical texts, Jesus was put to death because the message he brought threatened the powerful of his era. There are many more nuances than that, of course, and lots of ways one can spin the story to make one's point, but the simplest truth is that the gospel message was too toxic for the imperial stomach to bear.

So where does one begin to explore the story?

If we were to start with the opposition to Jesus, we

The biblical text

Matthew, Mark, and Luke seem to have used common sources, and give an overall "synopsis" of the life of Jesus; that's why they are generally referred to as the "synoptic gospels."

These three gospels are often lumped together because of their commonalities, as opposed to the fourth gospel, John, which is quite different. The stories in John are told more for their symbolic significance, and the author includes stories that are not found in the other three gospels.

Most scholars over the last 150 years or so have assumed that Mark's gospel was written first (sometime around 60–70 CE), and that Matthew and Luke used Mark as a primary source and then added things to that basic story. However, another school of thought suggests that Matthew and Luke could actually predate Mark, and that Mark stripped away a lot of the "fluff" in order to present a concise account of Jesus' life. We can't know for sure, which theory is correct. We do know, however, that of the four gospels included in the New Testament, John's was written last.

In this study, I use the gospel of Mark as the basis of the story and, for ease of use, I have included Mark's text taken from the *Common English Bible*. Occasionally, when there is a story that is unique to one of the other gospels, or where their version of a "shared" story differs significantly from Mark's version, I have reproduced the text from that gospel as well.

would have to start very early indeed. Mark 3:6, for example, tells of the Pharisees getting together with "the supporters of Herod to plan how to destroy Jesus," and Matthew 2 presents a ruthless King Herod who is bent on destroying the infant Jesus. Starting with the opposition to Jesus would make for a long study and would detract from the emphasis on the story of Jesus' death.

> Depending on your group and their familiarity with one another and their comfort with discussing biblical stories as myth, you may wish to read and explore Appendix A: Myth, Truth, and Fact.

The goal of this study is simply to engage you, the participant, in a deeper reading and exploration of this amazing story. What you take from it will depend on a number of factors – your previous faith commitment, your familiarity with the story, your understanding of the resurrection stories, and numerous others. There is simply too much in these texts to assume that everyone will come to the same conclusion about them and I am not seeking to make any single point. Perhaps, at the end of the day, the only thing we will all agree on is that this story is amazing, powerful, unique – and that the world was forever changed as a result of it.

Death of Jesus
FOR Progressive Christians

What if Christianity and salvation are really about transformation – the transformation of ourselves and of the world? – Marcus Borg, *The Heart of Christianity*

Palms and Conspiracy

The Palm Sunday story begins holy week for many Christians, and with it the annual exploration of the passion narrative. It is probably a familiar story to most of us: Jesus enters Jerusalem on the back of a donkey, people throw palm branches on the ground, the religious leaders scoff and get angry, and the people proclaim the words made famous in the communion liturgy: "Hosanna! Blessed is the one who comes in the name of God." That's the gist of it. But let's look at what the gospel writers say in more detail.

There are a lot of commonalities in the versions of the stories told in the synoptic gospels, which tells us that there is probably a basic set of facts behind the story. The differences, though present, do not place them in contradiction to each other. What's not so clear is that the entry of Jesus into Jerusalem that day is only half of the story.

I personally like to imagine Christ being one who'd enjoy a belly-busting laugh over a good, albeit clean, joke with his disciples, rather than always being the stoically serious kind of Saviour. – Frank Sterle, Jr., in "Letters to the Editor," *The Penticton Herald*

Mark 11:1–10

¹*When Jesus and his followers approached Jerusalem, they came to Bethphage and Bethany at the Mount of Olives. Jesus gave two disciples a task,* ²*saying to them, "Go into the village over there. As soon as you enter it, you will find tied up there a colt that no one has ridden. Untie it and bring it here.* ³*If anyone says to you, 'Why are you doing this?' say, 'Its master needs it, and he will send it back right away.'"*

⁴*They went and found a colt tied to a gate outside on the street, and they untied it.* ⁵*Some people standing around said to them, "What are you doing, untying the colt?"* ⁶*They told them just what Jesus said, and they left*

them alone. *7They brought the colt to Jesus and threw their clothes upon it, and he sat on it. 8Many people spread out their clothes on the road while others spread branches cut from the fields. 9Those in front of him and those following were shouting, "Hosanna! Blessings on the one who comes in the name of the Lord! 10Blessings on the coming kingdom of our ancestor David! Hosanna in the highest!"*

Mark 11:1 Jesus enters Jerusalem from the east, the direction of the Mount of Olives. This seemingly irrelevant directional detail is very important because the Roman governor, Pontius Pilate, entered Jerusalem from the west that same day. Jesus is riding a donkey, surrounded by a crowd that undoubtedly included a number of "misfits" – women, children, differently-abled people, and tax collectors among others; in short, riff raff. Pilate's procession, on the other hand, would have been mighty in number and power, proclaiming empire with every chariot, sword, shield, and soldier. The two processions are diametrically opposed, and we should assume that the entrance of Jesus on this particular day is not an accident, but was carefully planned.

■ Why might Jesus have planned to enter Jerusalem the same day as Pilate, from the opposite direction?
■ How might you have felt if you were part of the crowd with Jesus on that day?

Mark 11:2–3 The fact that Jesus tells the disciples what to do does not mean he is foretelling the future; Jesus knows that his message has challenged the authorities and that they are hostile to him. He sets things up quietly, presumably so that his plans do not get squashed before they come to fruition.

Mark 11:9 The people shout "Hosanna" which literally means "Save us!" but which came to be a statement of praise. The important point here is that you would only ask someone to save you if you believed that they actually could. They also mention David because for centuries the people had longed for a leader like David who they recalled as a great hero.

Comparing Matthew 21:1–11, Luke 19:29–40, and John 12:12–19

The text of Matthew follows Mark very closely. Matthew, however, includes reference to a "donkey" *and* a "colt" in verse 21:2, as if two animals are involved. Some have suggested that this is because Matthew – who is referencing both Zechariah 9:9 and Isaiah 62:11 in this one "saying" – does not understand the quotation from Zechariah 9:9, which says, in part, "he is riding on an ass, on a colt, the offspring of a donkey." Zechariah probably only means one animal and is using a bit of hyperbole in his writing, but one *could* see in this a reference to two animals. It may also be that Matthew intends to portray the entry into Jerusalem as a "living prophecy," since it was a common literary practice to have a character in a story act out a prophecy (Isaiah 62:11/Zechariah 9:9), essentially turning it into a "living," dramatic event. The fact that Zechariah referred to a colt emphasizes the lowliness of the king, who is clearly displaying humility by this act. This may be something that Matthew wants us to take from the story, or it may simply reflect the fact that Matthew likes to quote from the Hebrew scriptures.

Matthew 21:11 adds a brief conversation, noting that the whole city was stirred up. This gives Matthew an additional opportunity to identify Jesus and his importance.

The main difference between Luke's account (Luke 19:29–40) and Mark's version is that Luke reports the

Pharisees scolding Jesus, asking him to tell his disciples to be quiet. Jesus responds that even if the people are quiet, the stones will proclaim the message. In other words, you can't stop the inevitable – God's love is being proclaimed, and if you stop one source, the proclamation will simply come from somewhere else. This has strong overtones, because it could be taken a step further to mean "you can kill me, but there are countless others who will keep spreading the same message."

John's version of this story (John 12:12–19) does not include any mention of plans being made beforehand, but simply begins with a crowd going to meet Jesus, waving palm branches. The implication is that Jesus mounts the donkey in response to the people, suggesting this is not a pre-planned event. Also, John does not tell us from which direction Jesus enters from the city. Does John not want to draw any parallels to Pilate? We can't know for sure. Also, in John, the disciples do not understand what is going on. It is only after the resurrection, as they are trying to figure things out, that they piece this day together, and say "Oh yeah!"

Perhaps the most significant difference between the accounts is that John says that the people are praising Jesus because he raised Lazarus from the dead (John 12:17–19). The author also has the Pharisees say amongst themselves that they have accomplished nothing, that all of their attempts to thwart Jesus have failed, and that the whole world is following Jesus now.

■ What do you make of the various conversations that occur after Jesus arrives in Jerusalem?
■ Why do you think each gospel writer included the piece they did (or didn't include, in the case of Mark)?

Luke 19:41–44

⁴¹As Jesus came to the city and observed it, he wept over it. ⁴²He said, "If only you knew on this of all days the things that lead to peace. But now they are hidden from your eyes. ⁴³The time will come when your enemies will build fortifications around you, encircle you, and attack you from all sides. ⁴⁴They will crush you completely, you and the people within you. They won't leave one stone on top of another within you, because you didn't recognize the time of your gracious visit from God."

This passage is unique to Luke and indicates Jesus' compassion for the people of the city of Jerusalem. Some think Luke is inserting into the narrative a description of what occurred just prior to the writing of this gospel, when Jerusalem was conquered and destroyed by Rome. Others simply see Jesus observing that the people are living in the dark, and will reap the natural consequences.

Mark 11:11, 15–19

¹¹Jesus entered Jerusalem and went into the temple. After he looked around at everything, because it was already late in the evening, he returned to Bethany with the Twelve.

¹⁵They came into Jerusalem. After entering the temple, he threw out those who were selling and buying there. He pushed over the tables used for currency exchange and the chairs of those who sold doves. ¹⁶He didn't allow anyone to carry anything through the temple. ¹⁷He taught them, "Hasn't it been written, My house will be called a house of prayer for all nations? *But you've turned it into* a hideout for crooks."

¹⁸The chief priests and legal experts heard this and tried to find a way to destroy him. They regarded him as dangerous because the whole crowd was enthralled at his teaching. ¹⁹*When it was evening, Jesus and his disciples went outside the city.*

Mark 11:11 Mark tells us that Jesus, upon entering Jerusalem, spent the night before taking action in the temple, suggesting some pre-planning on Jesus' part.

Mark 11:15–17 Jesus goes to the temple, overturns the tables of those who changed money, and threw out those who were selling things. Jesus is not inside the temple building, as illustrations tend to depict, but is in the "court of Gentiles" – inside the outer walls, but in an open area. Buying and trading took place here, to enable the main temple actions of offering sacrifice. One could not use Roman currency (which had a "graven image" of the emperor) inside the temple, so one had to exchange this for acceptable currency, which was the Jewish and Tyrian shekel. Similarly, people needed animals to sacrifice, and doves were the traditional sacrifice of the poor. Consequently, note that Jesus is driving out people who seem to be undertaking fairly innocent transactions, which are necessary simply for people to meet religious requirements. Could it be, then, that Jesus' anger is directed first and foremost against those religious requirements? We tend to turn this into an image of Jesus driving out those who were cheating or gaining financially, but in fact he seems more intent on destroying the entire temple cult.

Mark 11:18 Matthew offers a short piece showing the response of the religious leadership to Jesus' actions. Mark tells us that the leadership "tried to find a way to destroy Jesus."

■ What point might Jesus be making in driving out the money changers and dove sellers?
■ People often refer to those whom Jesus drives out as the "money lenders" implying that this is a challenge to the modern institution of banking. However, there would be no role for money lenders in this story; the Greek term simply means those who exchanged money. Why might we shift this focus?
■ What kind of statement is Jesus making about the religious establishment in general?

Comparing Matthew 21:12–13, Luke 19:45–48, and John 2:14–17

Matthew and Luke essentially copy Mark, though Matthew's version is shorter and does not include the priests' plot against Jesus. Luke includes the plot to destroy Jesus, but adds that this plan is thwarted – temporarily at least – because Jesus had the support of the people. The actions of Jesus in John's version parallel Matthew and Luke, with small differences in detail (Jesus fashions a whip of chords, for example). In John 2:16–17, Jesus yells at the dove sellers, but instead of using the quotation from Jeremiah 7:11 that the other gospels employ ("you have made it a hideout for crooks") he uses a softer accusation: "Don't make my father's house a place of business." At this point, John says the disciples remember the scripture, "Passion [or zeal] for your house consumes me" (Psalm 69:9).

The biggest difference between John and the synoptic gospels, however, is that John places these events at the *beginning* of Jesus' ministry, not at the end. Scholars generally assume that all four gospels are referring to the same incident; John's decision to move it to the beginning of the gospel reminds us that it's often the *symbolism* of an event that John wants to emphasize.

The Jewish people believed that God lived in the temple, specifically in a central location known as the Holy of Holies. Jesus has frequently challenged this idea – suggesting that God is with(in) us wherever we are.

■ If you were a devout Jew and had been taught that the temple was the dwelling place of God, how might you have reacted to this action of Jesus?

■ If Jesus were to come into a place you consider sacred and "overturn tables," as it were, how might you respond?

■ What might Jesus be saying by doing this?

■ What point might John be wanting to make by placing this story near the beginning of his gospel?

■ Why might John have chosen to paint a more violent picture of Jesus in this story?

Mark 14:1–2

¹*It was two days before Passover and the Festival of Unleavened Bread. The chief priests and legal experts through cunning tricks were searching for a way to arrest Jesus and kill him. ²But they agreed that it shouldn't happen during the festival; otherwise, there would be an uproar among the people.*

Mark 14:1 Passover commemorates God's angel "passing over" the Hebrew families when it destroyed the first-born sons of the Egyptians. It is marked by eating bread with no leaven in it, a reminder that the Jews had to flee Egypt quickly, before their bread could rise – hence the two different names (Passover/Feast of Unleavened Bread). Passover is by far the most important of all annual Jewish festivals.

Mark 14:1–2 The chief priests and legal experts plot against Jesus; however, they concede that they should *not* do this during Passover, as the crowd is large and supportive of Jesus.

Matthew 26:1-5, Luke 22:1–2

In Matthew's version, Jesus predicts his own arrest and refers to himself as "the Human One." Earlier traditions translate this as "Son of Man." Matthew 26:3 adds the note that the chief priests are meeting at the home of the high priest, which suggests this is a more important gathering.

Luke 22:2 says, "The chief priests and the legal experts were looking for a way to kill Jesus, *because* [emphasis mine] they were afraid of the people," whereas Mark and Matthew say the opposite: the enemies of Jesus were plotting but *refrained* from acting out of fear.

In other words, two gospels tells us emphatically that the leadership do not want to kill Jesus until *after* Passover. However, Jesus has ridden boldly and publicly into Jerusalem and seems intent on teasing or provoking the leadership, virtually daring them to arrest him. He continues to speak and act proclaiming God's love even when he must know that this will lead to his death.

Mark 14:3–9

³Jesus was at Bethany visiting the house of Simon, who had a skin disease. During dinner, a woman came in with a vase made of alabaster and containing very expensive perfume of pure nard. She broke open the vase and poured the perfume on his head. ⁴Some grew angry. They said to each other, "Why waste the perfume? ⁵This perfume could have been sold for almost a year's pay and the money given to the poor." And they scolded her.

⁶Jesus said, "Leave her alone. Why do you make trouble for her? She has done a good thing for me. ⁷You always have the poor with you; and whenever you want, you can do something good for them. But you won't always have me. ⁸She has done what she could. She has anointed my body ahead of time for burial. ⁹I tell you the truth that, wherever in the whole world the good news is announced, what she's done will also be told in memory of her."

Mark 14:3–9 This is a key story in the narrative and it often gets a little lost, perhaps because Jesus elevates an unnamed woman. It is also intriguing that the story appears here in Mark, and also in Matthew and John, but not Luke, who tells a similar story much earlier in his gospel. There are enough differences in Luke's version that some scholars think it may refer to a different event. At the very least, Luke presents it as a teachable moment, an opportunity for Jesus to offer a parable, and does not use it as an element of the passion story.

Mark 14:3 We are told at the outset that Simon, the one hosting this dinner, is not socially acceptable. To have a skin disease rendered one ritually unclean. On the other hand, the guests are reclining at table, implying that this is a special meal. Simon has money, but his money cannot buy him social acceptance. The presence of Jesus, however, seems to have given him an acceptance that the religious rulers would not.

Mark 14:3 The woman is unnamed and, presumably, unknown. There is absolutely nothing to suggest that she is Mary Magdalene, although a rather strong tradition has tried to claim that over the years. Normally, men and women did not dine together, so the presence of the woman could suggest that Jesus has asked Simon break the rules; alternatively it suggests that she is someone who would not normally have been welcome – in other

words, a street woman or a sex-trade worker. This seems to "up the ante" of her acts. In any event, the woman anoints Jesus' head, a sign of honour.

Mark 14:4 Those who are gathered immediately grow angry, appalled that this woman has "wasted" this perfume, worth about a year's wages (three hundred *denaria*; a *denarius* was equal to a day's pay).

Mark 14:5 Jesus intervenes, telling them to leave her alone, pointing out that she has done a good thing by anointing him. After all, he says – and this is a harsh rebuke – they could help the poor anytime, implying that they don't do that much, and now are trying to cry foul. Jesus will have none of it.

Jesus points out that this unnamed woman has anointed him for burial, clearly foreshadowing what is to come. Then, in powerful words, Jesus proclaims that "wherever in the whole world the good news is announced, what she's done will also be told in memory of her."

Comparing Matthew 26:6–13, John 12:1–8, and Luke

Matthew's version of this story is virtually identical to Mark's, with only small variations present in the details: it is "the disciples" who get angry; Jesus doesn't hear their talk but simply "knows what they are thinking."

Although the gist of John's story is the same as we find in Mark and Matthew, many of the details have shifted. The setting here is completely different, this time taking place at the home of Lazarus whom Jesus had just a moment before raised from the dead. It is not an unnamed woman but one of the hosts, Mary, who anoints Jesus, and this time she anoints his feet, a standard act of welcome and hospitality. However, to use three-quarters of a pound of expensive perfume is outrageous. John is eager to employ symbolic meaning whenever he can. It is doubtful that anyone would have used such a vast amount of perfume, but John wants to emphasize that anointing/glorifying Jesus has no limits. Finally, it is Judas who complains about the "waste." John also adds the parenthetical note that Judas didn't really care about the poor, and was a thief anyway.

> Matthew and Mark tell us that Jesus said this story would be told in memory of this woman whenever the good news is shared.
> ■ How familiar are you with this story?
> ■ Why would this woman's story be important to the spreading of the good news?

Mark 14:10–11

[10]Judas Iscariot, one of the Twelve, went to the chief priests to give Jesus up to them. [11]When they heard it, they were delighted and promised to give him money. So he started looking for an opportunity to turn him in.

Mark 14:10–11 We move now from the amazing story of a woman anointing Jesus with an extremely expensive perfume to the story of one of Jesus' own disciples, Judas Iscariot, seeking to turn Jesus in. The contrast is huge and intentional on the part of most of the gospel writers. The woman is just someone from the crowd or those who are gathered, who wants to honour Jesus; the man is one of the inner circle, a disciple, who is willing to turn Jesus in. This needs to be seen as well against the backdrop of Passover, a great family celebration. Jesus has made a point of celebrating Passover with a "family" he has made up of his disciples. Judas' betrayal of Jesus

is all the greater because of the shame involved in turning in a member of one's own family.

Mark 14:10 "Iscariot" is thought by most scholars to mean simply that Judas is from Kerioth.

Matthew 26:14–16 and Luke 22:3–6

While Matthew's story is almost verbatim the same as Mark's, he makes a couple significant changes. Matthew removes the reference to the chief priests being "delighted" at Judas' proposal, but he includes the mention of 30 pieces of silver. While we cannot know the value of this money for certain, generally it is thought to have been of significantly less value than the perfume that was used to anoint Jesus. However, the term has entered into our modern usage, and, frequently, a reference to 30 pieces of silver is seen as a sign of betrayal. At a United Nations conference on climate change, the representative from Tuvalu, a South Pacific nation that is rapidly disappearing due to climate change, stated, "It looks like we are being offered 30 pieces of silver to betray our people and our future...but our future is not for sale."

In Matthew and Mark, Judas initiates the action, going to the chief priests and asking what they might give him to turn Jesus over. Luke, presumably feeling a need to explain this bizarre change in the behaviour of one of the disciples, involves "the Accuser" – the appropriate translation for the word *satan*. "Satan" in Jewish literature is one who takes an opposing position to God, the kind of individual who might say "I'm going to play devil's advocate for a moment." Used in Luke's account, it has the effect of softening what Judas has done. "How could he help it?" one might ask, "Satan was in him."

■ Why do you think Judas betrayed Jesus?
■ What might the gospel writers be trying to say in contrasting Judas' behaviour with the woman from the previous story, who anointed Jesus?

Death of Jesus

FOR
Progressive
Christians

Closing Thoughts

So the story has begun with great fanfare and hope in the story of Palm Sunday and its bold – some would say brazen – act of defying Rome. However, the narrative has plummeted rather quickly as Judas moves toward betrayal, and we clearly see signs of impending doom.

In the face of all this, I invite you to consider some people – one group and two individuals. In the first instance, imagine the crowd that swept Jesus into Jerusalem. What feelings might they be having? What might change for them as the story progresses?

Next, think of the unnamed woman (or, if you prefer, think of her as Mary of Bethany) who anoints Jesus, and of Judas, the one who sets out to betray him. What might they feel as the story continues on from here?

Lastly, consider yourself in all this. Where might you be? What risks might be associated with placing yourself at certain parts of the story?

Table and Garden

The portions of the story we explore in this session are a little calmer than the rest. We read of a meal (the Last Supper) and of Jesus at prayer in the Garden of Gethsemane. They are not the most peaceful of stories certainly – Jesus speaks of sacrifice and betrayal at the supper, and the disciples basically leave him to suffer in the Garden – but still this can be seen as the proverbial calm before the storm.

Mark 14:12–17

12On the first day of the Festival of Unleavened Bread, when the Passover lamb was sacrificed, the disciples said to Jesus, "Where do you want us to prepare for you to eat the Passover meal?"

13He sent two of his disciples and said to them, "Go into the city. A man carrying a water jar will meet you. Follow him. 14Wherever he enters, say to the owner of the house, 'The teacher asks, "Where is my guest room where I can eat the Passover meal with my disciples?"' 15He will show you a large room upstairs already furnished. Prepare for us there." 16The disciples left, came into the city, found everything just as he had told them, and they prepared the Passover meal.

17That evening, Jesus arrived with the Twelve.

Mark 14:12 This meal takes place on the day when the Passover lambs were sacrificed – that is Thursday night (hence the church's tradition of observing this meal on Holy or Maundy Thursday).

Mark 14:13–15 Jesus sends two disciples into town to make arrangements. Jesus clearly knows the place where they are going to meet, and we need not read a lot of secrecy or special knowledge into this. They ask where they should go, and Jesus says, "go into town – there's someone who will meet you and he'll show you the place." That Jesus knows the place ahead of time is not significant. It is possible that Jesus wants to keep the location secret because he knows of the dangers involved, although we cannot know this for certain.

Mark 14:15 The room is described as "already furnished." We need to remember that this means there would be a lot of cushions on the floor, and possibly (but not necessarily) a low table (see box "The Last Supper" on p. 31).

Matthew 26:17–20, Luke 22:7–14,

Matthew's version of the story (Matthew 26:17–20) is shorter than Mark's, but essentially covers the same material. Matthew 26:20 says, "he took his place at the table." The word "table" does not appear in the Greek text, but shows up in several English translations, some going so far as to say Jesus "sat at table" which is incorrect. Jews always reclined to eat the Passover feast. While this was generally a Roman custom, they adopted it for this meal as a way of celebrating the freedom given by God to live life in a more leisurely manner.

Luke's account (Luke 22:7–14) essentially blends Mark's and Matthew's versions, keeping the length of Mark, but adding Matthew's closing line about taking a place at table. The only other real difference is that Jesus asks for *"the* guestroom"; in Mark, Jesus asks for *"my* guestroom." There is probably little significance in the change, although Luke may be wanting to emphasize that Jesus has this already planned out.

Footwashing - John 13:1-20

It has been said that the entire gospel of John is a commentary or sermon on the Last Supper, and yet the traditional elements (sharing of bread and cup) that we associate with that meal are not present in John. Instead, John offers a unique story about Jesus washing the disciples' feet. Almost as a tease, Jesus returns to the table afterwards (verse 12), suggesting that the Last Supper might have been going on, but John makes only passing reference to it.

The statement that the devil had "entered" or "provoked" Judas (verse 2) is significant, because Jesus still includes him in the community of disciples, even though he knows that Judas will betray him. Jesus takes on the form of a slave - no robes, a linen towel tied around his waist - and gets down on his knees to wash the disciples' feet. This astonishing act surprises the disciples, who protest, but Jesus persists.

The act of washing feet was a basic act of hospitality, akin to taking someone's coat when they come to your home, and offering them a cup of coffee. More than the physical cleansing of the feet, it was a way of saying that the person was welcome in your home. Given that the provision of hospitality was the greatest commandment in Judaism, this is key. Jesus - on God's behalf - welcomes us. Jesus points out the example he has offered: "If I, your Lord and teacher, have washed your feet, you too must wash each other's feet." More than anything else, this illustrates to the disciples that they are to be servants of one another.

■ What do you make of the symbolism of this act, that Jesus offers a humble act of hospitality on God's behalf?

■ How do you feel welcomed by God?

[18]During the meal, Jesus said, "I assure you that one of you will betray me – someone eating with me."

[19]Deeply saddened, they asked him, one by one, "It's not me, is it?"

[20]Jesus answered, "It's one of the Twelve, one who is dipping bread with me into this bowl. [21]The Human One goes to his death just as it is written about him. But how terrible it is for that person who betrays the Human One! It would have been better for him if he had never been born."

Mark 14:18–19 Jesus tells the disciples, in the midst of the Passover meal, that one of them will betray him; their response is quite predictable, as they all ask, "It's not me, is it?"

Mark 14:20 Rather than use utensils, people ate with their hands and then mopped things up with pieces of bread. Thus, there is nothing unusual about "dipping bread." The significance of the reference is simply that Jesus is speaking about someone who is either sitting right beside him, or is symbolically one of his closest friends – either definition could apply to Judas.

Comparing Matthew 26:21–25, Luke 22:21–23, John 13:21–30

Once again, Matthew's account (Matthew 26:21–25) is very similar to Mark's version. Matthew's account differs from Mark, however, in that the disciple who will betray Jesus is actually named in verse 25: "Now Judas, who would betray him, replied, 'It's not me, is it, Rabbi?'" In Matthew's gospel, the title "Rabbi" is used by non-Christians. Matthew seems to be making a stinging commentary on Judas by having him use this term.

Luke's version of the story (Luke 22:21–23) is quite

a bit shorter than Matthew's and Mark's. Luke seems loathe to assign guilt, blame, or shame to the disciples, and so the story here is less accusatory and ends with the disciples arguing amongst themselves about who it could be.

First, it's important to note that the timing of the meal in John's version (John 13:21–30) is different, most significantly in that it doesn't happen on the Passover, but the night before. John includes details in his account that are not present in Mark, Luke, and Matthew, or that differ. For example, when Jesus foretells his betrayal, Peter nods discreetly at one of the other disciples to ask Jesus who the guilty party might be. Rather than say "the one who dips their bread with me" Jesus is entirely in control of this scenario, and says "the person to whom I will give this piece of bread." The phrase "the one whom Jesus loved" is also unique to John's gospel, and is thought to refer to the disciple John.

■ How might you feel if you were one of the disciples sitting at table with Jesus at this moment?
■ The differences in the stories are striking, perhaps enough to question their factuality. Does one seem more believable to you than another? Why?

Mark 14:22–25

²²While they were eating, Jesus took bread, blessed it, broke it, and gave it to them, and said, "Take; this is my body." ²³He took a cup, gave thanks, and gave it to them, and they all drank from it. ²⁴He said to them, "This is my blood of the covenant, which is poured out for many. ²⁵I assure you that I won't drink wine again until that day when I drink it in a new way in God's kingdom."

The Last Supper

Leonardo da Vinci's painting "The Last Supper" is so indelibly emblazoned in our minds that we assume this image represents the way the meal must have taken place, but it does not.

Da Vinci's "Last Supper" was not immediately appreciated by the folks he painted it for. It appears in the dining area of a monastery, painted on the wall. As an indication of how much it was under-appreciated, at one point the monks cut a door into the wall, removing Jesus' legs!

Da Vinci did something quite extraordinary by placing the scene in what was for him a local and modern setting – an Italian house. The painting is quite large and all the disciples are seated along one side. This leaves the monks, who would have dined at the monastery, symbolically on the other side of the table, facing the scene. The painting depicts the moment when Jesus says "one of you will betray me." This invited the monks who were dining – and all who have viewed the painting since – to contemplate Jesus' statement and to join the disciples in their collective gulp: "It's not me, is it?"

■ How does it sit with you, knowing that the image so many of us have of the Last Supper is not biblically accurate?

■ Is Jesus' statement ("one of you will betray me") something you contemplate today?

Death of Jesus
FOR Progressive Christians

[Body and blood] are reminders that Jesus died a violent death, killed by the powers that rule this world. This sacrament is about becoming one with this Jesus. It is about joining our lives to his life, our passion to his passion.
– Marcus Borg, *Speaking Christian*

The story presented here is heavily influenced by the practices of the early church, as described in 1 Corinthians 11:23–26. We know that there were in the early church a variety of different forms of the "Lord's supper," as they called it. The one described in 1 Corinthians largely became the "norm."

Another form of communion

Among the many practices of communion in the early church, one that stands out involved three cups. First, one would drink from a cup of water, symbolic of baptism. It was considered a ritual of cleansing oneself from the inside out. The second cup was wine, reminiscent of Jesus' meal with the disciples. The last cup held milk mixed with honey, reminding the participant of the hope we have as Christians that God will indeed lead us into a land flowing with milk and honey.
■ What do you think of this style of communion?

Mark 14:22 Jesus took bread, blessed it ... This is not quite accurate, as Jews did not bless objects, but rather blessed God for providing the objects. It's essentially like our practice of saying grace before a meal.

Mark 14:22 Jesus tells the disciples that this bread is "my body." Given that the bread represented God freeing the people from slavery, this could be seen as Jesus saying, "God will use *me* to help effect your (ongoing) liberation."

Mark 14:24 Jesus' statement about drinking his blood is a curious one, for Jews believed it was not kosher to touch blood, or to consume it, which is why animals must be slaughtered in a certain way in order to be considered kosher. Accordingly, Jesus' statement is very radical – a challenge, perhaps, to the very system that required obedience to particular laws in order to be included in the distinct and chosen people of God. Perhaps Jesus is saying that those laws do not matter any longer.

Mark 14:25 Jesus states – albeit in a roundabout way – that he will drink wine again in the realm of God, a bold affirmation that he anticipates being present in some form with the disciples long after this night. How we understand this may depend on our understanding of resurrection and of Christ's presence, but there can be no denying that Jesus expected major changes to occur.

Comparing Matthew 26:28, Luke 22: 15–20

Matthew's story (Matthew 26:26–29) is a close parallel to Mark, although he adds the unique line that Jesus' blood is poured out "for forgiveness."

Luke's version veers from Mark and Matthew, not least with the oddity of including two cups. In Luke 22:17, the first time Jesus shares a cup, he simply invites the disciples to share it amongst themselves, and points out that he will drink it again when God's realm has come. In Luke 22:20, with the second cup, Jesus tells the disciples that this is the new covenant in Jesus' blood, poured out for them. Scholars have put forward a variety of explanation for the difference, ranging from some mystical theological point Luke might be trying to make, to suggesting that he simply misunderstood the story he was originally given.

> ■ There are many ways to understand the meaning(s) of what we have come to know as holy communion. What are some of the meanings/symbolisms for you?

Luke 22:24–30

²⁴*An argument broke out among the disciples over which one of them should be regarded as the greatest.*

²⁵*But Jesus said to them, "The kings of the Gentiles rule over their subjects, and those in authority over them are called 'friends of the people.'* ²⁶*But that's not the way it will be with you. Instead, the greatest among you must become like a person of lower status and the leader like a servant.* ²⁷*So which one is greater, the one who is seated at the table or the one who serves at the table? Isn't it the one who is seated at the table? But I am among you as one who serves.*

²⁸*"You are the ones who have continued with me in my trials.* ²⁹*And I confer royal power on you just as my Father granted royal power to me.* ³⁰*Thus you will eat and drink at my table in my kingdom, and you will sit on thrones overseeing the twelve tribes of Israel.*

Luke is unique in placing this story at this point in the narrative. The other gospels include it much earlier in the ministry of Jesus, but Luke has placed it at the end of the meal. Thus, a powerful contrast is made between those who *think* they are important, and those who really are. Power, Jesus points out, rests in one's ability to serve others. This idea is key throughout Jesus' ministry, but seems a little stronger when spoken here, at the point he has just symbolically offered up his body and blood. "The greatest among you must be a servant" and "I am among you as one who serves" define much of Jesus' understanding of human relations, and will come into play in the next several hours as Jesus is challenged and questioned by those who think they have authority, but who seem no match for this one they regard as being beneath them.

²⁶*After singing songs of praise, they went out to the Mount of Olives.*

²⁷*Jesus said to them, "You will all falter in your faithfulness to me. It is written,* I will hit the shepherd, and the sheep will go off in all directions. ²⁸*But after I'm raised up, I will go before you to Galilee."*

²⁹*Peter said to him, "Even if everyone else stumbles, I won't."*

³⁰*But Jesus said to him, "I assure you that on this very night, before the rooster crows twice, you will deny me three times."*

³¹*But Peter insisted, "If I must die alongside you, I won't deny you." And they all said the same thing.*

Mark 14:26 The Passover meal ends with the traditional singing of hymns of praise, and the disciples head off to the Mount of Olives. All four gospels record the scene of Peter swearing that he will stick with Jesus to the end, and of Jesus pointing out that he will not. The details differ, but the point of the story is the same in all the gospels.

Mark 14:30 Mark includes the odd phrase "before the rooster crows twice, you will deny me three times." Most scholars see this simply as an interesting turn of phrase, rather like the rhyme that results with slightly archaic English: "before the rooster crows twice, you will deny me thrice." The same play on words exists in Greek.

Comparing Matthew 26:30-35, Luke 22:31-34, John 13:36-38

In Matthew's version (Matthew 26:30-35), Jesus offers an encouraging note about resurrection in verse 32. In verse 35, *all* the disciples, not just Peter, agree that they will stick with Jesus.

BIBLE STUDY

**Death of
Jesus**

FOR
Progressive
Christians

Luke's story (Luke 22:31–34) takes place not on the way to the Mount of Olives, but back at the dinner. Although Jesus had given Peter his new name, which means "rock," in verse 31 he reverts to calling him by his former name "Simon," Hebrew for "shifting sands." In the next verse, Luke adds a hint of forgiveness, with Jesus saying "when you have returned, strengthen your brothers and sisters."

Although the setting of John's version (John 13:36–38) is different yet again, and the conversation begins with Peter asking, "Where are you going?" the end result is remarkably similar.

Luke 22:35–38

[35]*Jesus said to them, "When I sent you out without a wallet, bag, or sandals, you didn't lack anything, did you?"*

They said, "Nothing."

[36]*Then he said to them, "But now, whoever has a wallet must take it, and likewise a bag. And those who don't own a sword must sell their clothes and buy one.* [37]*I tell you that this scripture must be fulfilled in relation to me: And he was counted among criminals. Indeed, what's written about me is nearing completion."*

[38]*They said to him, "Lord, look, here are two swords."*

He replied, "Enough of that!"

This story is unique to Luke and serves as a tragic prediction of what is about to unfold. The disciples, who have been following Jesus for several years and learning ways of relating among themselves and with others that follow lines of peace, hospitality, and affirmation, are now being told that they will be shunned and rejected. They'll need to pay their own way; they'll need to defend themselves. This sounds like something quite different than what they signed up for! Yet it is the way of the world for all who seek to follow paths that run counter to the status quo – they are shunned, rejected, shamed, ridiculed, and worse. Jesus will model that in the next 24 hours, and his followers have experienced it throughout all of history ever since.

Mark 14:32–42

32Jesus and his disciples came to a place called Gethsemane. Jesus said to them, "Sit here while I pray." 33He took Peter, James, and John along with him. He began to feel despair and was anxious. 34He said to them, "I'm very sad. It's as if I'm dying. Stay here and keep alert." 35Then he went a short distance farther and fell to the ground. He prayed that, if possible, he might be spared the time of suffering. 36He said, "Abba, Father, for you all things are possible. Take this cup of suffering away from me. However – not what I want but what you want."

37He came and found them sleeping. He said to Peter, "Simon, are you asleep? Couldn't you stay alert for one hour? 38Stay alert and pray so that you won't give in to temptation. The spirit is eager, but the flesh is weak."

39Again, he left them and prayed, repeating the same words. 40And, again, when he came back, he found them sleeping, for they couldn't keep their eyes open, and they didn't know how to respond to him. 41He came a third time and said to them, "Will you sleep and rest all night? That's enough! The time has come for the Human One to be betrayed into the hands of sinners. 42Get up! Let's go! Look, here comes my betrayer."

Mark 14:32 Gethsemane is a garden at the foot of the Mount of Olives, a significant site for Jews since long before the time of Jesus. Jews believed that when the Messiah came he would begin to resurrect people at the Mount of Olives, and thus to be buried there meant you

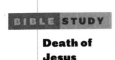

Death of Jesus

FOR Progressive Christians

In his prayer he learns to pray to a Creator God as "Abba," or "Papa," thus personalizing as no religion ever had the intimate bond between creature and Creator.
– Matthew Fox, *Original Blessing*

would be resurrected sooner. Some of this symbolism may be present in Jesus choosing this garden for prayer, or it may simply be that it was a convenient location.

Mark 14:36 Mark is unique among the gospels in having Jesus begin his prayer with the word *"Abba"* to refer to God. This word means more than just "father"; it is closer to "papa" or "dad." It is a highly personal term, a diminutive of the Hebrew and Aramaic *"ab,"* which means father. The significance of using *abba* is not that it defines God as male, but rather that Jesus would use such a tender, close term. There is no rigid formality here; this is Jesus talking very closely and personally to the one he has known as his dad, whom we can readily recognize as being much closer than someone we would call "Father."

Mark 14:36 Jesus ends his prayer – in all three synoptic gospels – with the bold statement "not what I want, but what you want" (or a variation thereof).

Mark 14:37 Jesus takes Peter, James, and John with him when he goes to pray. These three figure prominently also in the story of the transfiguration, suggesting that Mark may have been wanting to make a link for the reader – this is another moment when Jesus will be recognized as the Christ, as God's beloved. This is intriguing, because the prayer that Jesus utters in these two gospels might appear to show weakness – or simply incredible honesty.

Mark 14:38 The line "the spirit is eager (willing), but the flesh is weak" was a common expression, similar to our modern "my heart says yes, but my feet say no."

Mark 14:39 Jesus prays three times, and after each finds the disciples sleeping, seemingly oblivious to all that

was about to take place. Note that in this version of the prayer, Jesus simply says, "take this away from me." One could see here a sign of weakness – Jesus prays to God to release him from the inevitable, to allow him to sidestep the violence and suffering that are about to come. However, Jesus adds the line "not my will, but yours" – a clear indication that he is prepared to follow God's lead and direction, and to follow through.

It is important to note that this prayer does not inherently mean that it is God's will that Jesus die. We tend to jump to that conclusion based on traditional understandings and interpretations of the text, but it does not say that. Jesus' submission to God's will here is simply a realization that he will continue on the path that has begun. God's will for all humanity is life – blessed, full, and abundant life. It is the will of the *people* in this story that Jesus be killed, *not* the will of God.

Mark 14:42 The betrayer is at hand. The end is now coming, and the opportunity for Jesus to depart, to step away, to run and hide, has gone. Jesus will now take whatever the world seeks to throw at him; he will stop at nothing to continue proclaiming God's love for all creation.

Comparing Matthew 26:36–44, Luke 22:39–46, and John 18:1

Matthew follows Mark's account very closely, with a few small changes. Matthew refers to James and John by their father's name, calling them the sons of Zebedee (vs. 37). Rather than using the very intimate term "Abba" as in Mark, Matthew uses "My Father" (vs. 39). And to Jesus' simple line "take this cup of suffering away from me" in Mark, Matthew adds "if it's possible," suggesting that it might be beyond God's ability to intervene, or that it might alter the course of history too significantly.

Again, as in several other places, Luke seems to have done some editing to the story told by Mark and Matthew. In Luke's version (Luke 22:39–46), Jesus goes off on his own, but remains close – although theoretically out of earshot (a "stone's throw" away) of the disciples. In verse 44, Luke writes, "His sweat became like drops of blood falling on the ground." It is vital to notice the use of the word "like" here, because it is a grammatical clue that this is a simile and not a statement of fact. Luke wants us to understand the earnestness and anguish of Jesus' prayer, and does so by saying he was sweating profusely – to the point that it was *like* drops of blood. Despite some portrayals (Mel Gibson's *The Passion of the Christ* being one example), Luke does *not* mean to imply that Jesus was actually bleeding.

John 18:1 contains no prayer or even reference to one, but simply tells us that Jesus and the disciples crossed the valley to a garden. John has dealt with many issues of Jesus' prayer previously, such as in John 12:27: "Now *I am deeply troubled.* What should I say? 'Father, save me from this time'? No, for this is the reason I have come to this time."

■ What do you make of Jesus' prayer?
■ Do you see Jesus' request to be set free from this suffering as a sign of weakness, or honesty, or something else?
■ How do you understand Jesus' statement "not my will, but yours, be done"?
■ What is your emotional reaction when you read of Jesus' commitment in the prayer in Gethsemane?

Closing Thoughts

Jesus seems to have ample opportunity to run away, or to hide, or to fade into the woodwork, or perhaps worst, to deny the path he is on. But he doesn't. Similarly, in Gethsemane, he prays for God's will to be done, not his own.

We could see in all of this an incredibly passive individual, one who has no sense of his inherent value. Or we could see an individual who is so heartily committed to the task of sharing God's love, with no conditions, that he is willing to sacrifice everything to do that. Nothing, not even death – or at this point in the story, the threat of death – will stop him.

Death of Jesus
FOR
Progressive
Christians

Arrest and Denial

Jesus has just completed his prayer in the Garden of Gethsemane when Judas appears with a group of others. Jesus is arrested.

This story appears in all four gospels, as will much of the remainder through the crucifixion, although with some obvious differences. Again, it is worth remembering that the differences in the details do not by and of themselves nullify the validity of the story. Imagine four individuals describing an event today: each will likely emphasize different aspects, and tell parts of their story differently, because they all want to make a specific point.

Mark 14:43–52

⁴³*Suddenly, while Jesus was still speaking, Judas, one of the Twelve, came with a mob carrying swords and clubs. They had been sent by the chief priests, legal experts, and elders.* ⁴⁴*His betrayer had given them a sign: "Arrest the man I kiss, and take him away under guard."*

⁴⁵*As soon as he got there, Judas said to Jesus, "Rabbi!" Then he kissed him.* ⁴⁶*Then they came and grabbed Jesus and arrested him.*

⁴⁷*One of the bystanders drew a sword and struck the high priest's slave and cut off his ear.* ⁴⁸*Jesus responded, "Have you come with swords and clubs to arrest me, like an outlaw?* ⁴⁹*Day after day, I was with you, teaching in the temple, but you didn't arrest me. But let the scriptures be fulfilled."* ⁵⁰*And all his disciples left him and ran away.* ⁵¹*One young man, a disciple, was wearing nothing but a linen cloth. They grabbed him,* ⁵²*but he left the linen cloth behind and ran away naked.*

Mark 14:43 Matthew, Mark, and John all present Judas at the head of a large crowd sent by the chief priests and elders of the people; Mark describes them as a "mob" which sounds a bit more sinister.

Mark 14:44–45 Judas greets Jesus with a kiss – a fairly standard greeting in that culture – a signal that he has prearranged with the ones who were sent to arrest Jesus. At this point, the conflict in the story is essentially confined to religion. Jesus is being challenged by his own faith community because the message he has brought – about God's unconditional love, and forgiveness, and of a preferential option for the poor and marginalized – is at odds with that of the religious leadership. It challenges the religion they are teaching, and thus threatens their position.

Mark 14:47–49 For information about the incident concerning the cutting off of someone's ear in all four gospels see p. 44.

Mark 14:50 Both Mark and Matthew tell us that all the disciples ran away at this point. Luke does not give us this story at all, perhaps being reluctant to portray the disciples in an unfavourable light.

Mark 14:51–52 Mark is unique in including this tiny story, and scholars are all over the map when it comes to deciding why it is there. Who is this young man? Is it the author, Mark, or someone else? Is it a follower of Jesus (as the *Common English Bible* suggests) or simply someone who followed Jesus or the crowd that night? Is his appearance after the flight of the disciples simply a literary device to suggest that everyone ran away, but one came back – rather like the ten lepers Jesus healed? Did

the young man run off and hide in a cave that became the tomb, and thus is he the young man of Mark 16:5, who greets the women on Easter morning – in new, almost regal clothing – and tells them that Jesus is risen?

All these possibilities and more are of interest, perhaps because of the oddity of the story. But we have no way of knowing what Mark intended.

All four gospels include the incident where someone cuts off the ear of one of the high priest's servants or slaves, although they all offer slightly different versions. The fact that they all include the story suggests two things: first, that it quite probably happened; and second, that there is undoubtedly some significance to it. First, let's look at the information they present in the chart opposite.

There is some disagreement over who drew their sword, but not over what happened next. Interestingly, Luke has Jesus heal the man. In Matthew, Luke and John, Jesus says, "Put your sword away." Clearly, Jesus doesn't want a violent response to his arrest. The synoptic gospels also have Jesus rather pointedly reminding the crowd that they have had numerous opportunities to arrest him, day after day, but have chosen night – as Luke says, "your time, when darkness rules."

John does not have this second response, but simply stretches out the first point – that the disciples should not try to avoid the inevitable.

Jesus' message throughout is clearly presented: the course of natural events in this story should not be stopped, and the people are clearly showing their cowardice.

■ What feelings does this story leave you with?

Comparing Matthew 26:47–56, Luke 22:47–53, John 18:2–12a

BIBLE STUDY

Death of Jesus

FOR Progressive Christians

Matthew's version of the story (Matthew 26:47–56) is largely the same as Mark's, although Matthew softens Mark's "mob" to "crowd." Matthew also has Jesus say, "do you think that I'm not able to ask my Father and he will send to me more than twelve battle groups of angels right away?" (vs. 53), but the point he is trying to make is the same as in Mark: these things are happening to fulfill scripture.

	Matthew	Mark	Luke	John
instigator	unnamed disciple	bystander	someone in crowd supporting Jesus	Simon Peter
slave's name	unknown	unknown	unknown	Malchus
Jesus' first response	"Put your sword away. Those who use the sword will die by the sword."		"Stop! No more of this." Touches ear and heals slave.	"Put your sword away."
Jesus' second response	"Have you come with swords and clubs to arrest me like a thief? Day after day I sat in the temple teaching but you didn't arrest me."	"Have you come with swords and clubs to arrest me, like an outlaw? Day after day, I was with you, teaching in the temple, but you didn't arrest me."	"Have you come with swords and clubs to arrest me, as though I were a thief? Day after day I was with you in the temple, but you didn't arrest me. But this is your time, when darkness rules."	"Am I not to drink the cup the Father has given me?"

Luke's version (Luke 22:47–53) does not say that the crowd was sent by the religious leaders, although it's clear from what happens afterwards, because it leads Jesus to the high priest and no Roman crowd would have done that.

In John 18:2–12a, rather than a "crowd" or a "mob," John refers to a "company," which was 600 soldiers – undoubtedly a gross exaggeration, but meant to emphasize the lunacy of sending a massive number of soldiers to arrest someone who was essentially a peasant. It is meant to indicate the irrational fear the authorities had – fear of a simple message about God's love!

One of the biggest differences in John's version comes at John 18:4–5, with Jesus going out to greet (confront?) Judas and the crowd. In presenting it this way, John depicts Jesus firmly in control of the situation, as if to say, "You may think you've got the upper hand, but you do not." To drive this home, when Jesus asks who they are looking for and they respond "Jesus the Nazarene," Jesus replies with a simple, and grammatically awkward, "I am." John clearly wants his readers to associate this with God's proclamation to Moses at the burning bush: "I am what I

The sword

Some scholars have pointed out that since the synoptic gospels present this day as being the first day of Passover, it would have been forbidden to carry weapons, leaving us to wonder how someone would have had a sword. Is this Mark and Luke's way of telling us that the crowd did not observe God's law, or cared little about the importance of Passover? If so, it is curious that Matthew presents the instigator as being one of the followers of Jesus – although not necessarily one of the Twelve – which could be an indication that this crowd, while claiming to arrest Jesus because they wished to protect the "purity" of their religious beliefs and practices, nonetheless didn't care about them that much.

■ What experiences have you had of people espousing religious beliefs, but not practicing them?

am" or "I will be what I will be." At this, the company (of 600 soldiers, remember) falls to the ground. Although highly unlikely under any circumstance, John clearly wanted readers to recognize who Jesus is – nothing less than God – and be overcome with awe, just like the soldiers. In John 18:12, rather than have the disciples leave, Jesus tells the authorities that if he is the one they are seeking, they should let the others go. Again, it is John's way of reminding us that Jesus is very much in control here.

> ■ What do you make of John's clear attempt here to show Jesus in control of the situation?
> ■ How do you respond to John's indication that Jesus is not merely human, but is in fact God? What do you make of the fact that only one gospel does this?

Mark 14:53–65

53They led Jesus away to the high priest, and all the chief priests, elders, and legal experts gathered. 54Peter followed him from a distance, right into the high priest's courtyard. He was sitting with the guards, warming himself by the fire. 55The chief priests and the whole Sanhedrin were looking for testimony against Jesus in order to put him to death, but they couldn't find any. 56Many brought false testimony against him, but they contradicted each other. 57Some stood to offer false witness against him, saying, 58"We heard him saying, 'I will destroy this temple, constructed by humans, and within three days I will build another, one not made by humans.'" 59But their testimonies didn't agree even on this point.

60Then the high priest stood up in the middle of the gathering and examined Jesus. "Aren't you going to respond to the testimony these people have brought against you?" 61But Jesus was silent and didn't answer. Again, the high priest asked, "Are you the Christ, the Son of the blessed one?"

⁶²*Jesus said, "I am. And you will see the Human One sitting on the right side of the Almighty and coming on the heavenly clouds."*

⁶³*Then the high priest tore his clothes and said, "Why do we need any more witnesses? ⁶⁴You've heard his insult against God. What do you think?"*

They all condemned him. "He deserves to die!"

⁶⁵*Some began to spit on him. Some covered his face and hit him, saying, "Prophesy!" Then the guards took him and beat him.*

We finish this session by moving into the trial of Jesus by the religious authorities, which will be followed by a political interrogation by the Roman authorities, ultimately resulting in Jesus' death. A number of curiosities are present in the religious trial, not the least of which being that, if the context were not so terrible, we might see it for the rather laughable affair that it is. These folks are intent on finding Jesus guilty of *something*, but they almost stumble over each other to find evidence, and cannot come up with much.

Mark 14:53 Mark does not identify the high priest, although it is generally accepted by both Jewish and Christian scholars that it was Caiaphas at this time. The truth of the matter, though, is that it doesn't really matter. Annas was appointed high priest in the year 6, and we know that the position of high priest was passed among a variety of men. Most significantly, for some 40 years it was held exclusively by Annas or members of his family – Caiaphas was his son-in-law. Usually, anyone in authority for that long has a tendency to become complacent at best, or corrupt at worst. Either can lead to a rather fanatical desire to preserve one's status at all costs, and that would be in keeping with a priesthood (along with its cronies) bent on stamping out anyone who might appear to challenge their authority and grip on power. Jesus fits this bill perfectly.

Mark 14:54 Peter follows behind Jesus and the crowd right into the high priest's courtyard. He wants to know what is going on; he also, however, does not want to be found out.

Mark 14:55–59 Mark tells us that the council was seeking testimony against Jesus in order to put him to death. In a rather ridiculous scenario, they cannot seem to find anything, and the few witnesses they do find who said Jesus was going to destroy the temple and rebuild it could not even get their stories straight.

Mark 14:61 Jesus remains silent in response to the initial accusations brought against him. One clear possibility for this is that he finds the charges so ludicrous they

The temple

The concern about the destruction of the temple may have had greater impact on the ones accusing Jesus, and/or for the early church, than it does for us. The temple was understood as the place where God lived, in the Holy of Holies. (This will figure again at the time of Jesus' crucifixion.) For the Jews, the central place to practice their religion, beyond the home, was the temple. By threatening to destroy it, is the author saying that we do not need a *place* to worship God? What might this mean for those who make their living – the priests – through the sacrifices offered there?

Is the author saying that God comes to us, or (worse still in his accusers' minds) that people do not need the priests at all? Is the author in saying the temple will be destroyed, speaking of overthrowing established religion, which had become a burden for many? Furthermore, is the statement about the building of another temple, without the aid of human hands, a way of saying that the real dwelling place of God is among the people, or that Christ (and consequently the church) controls access to God, rendering the priests redundant?

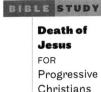

[The Pharisees and Sadducees] made the mistake of believing they had a right to stand between God and God's people – when no such permission was given to them and no request made of them.
– John Pavlovitz, via the Internet

are not worth speaking to. The authorities despise Jesus because he speaks of God's love of bringing in those who have been pushed to the edges of society, and of harmony among those who have historically been at odds with each other. Yet none of these are punishable offences, so in order to get rid of him they need to find other, more damning evidence.

The high priest takes a gamble and bluntly asks Jesus if he is the Christ, the Messiah, the son of the living God. Jesus offers a fairly brusque "I am" which may be a simple "yes," or may be meant to conjure God's declaration in the burning bush (although the context for this is not as strong in Mark as in John).

In each of the synoptic gospels, Jesus supports his answer with a quotation blending Psalm 110:1 and Daniel 7:13–14: "From now on, the Human One will be seated on the right side of the power of God." It is an interesting way of wresting power away from the high priest, and stating (albeit subtly) that Jesus has the real authority here.

Mark 14:63 In the synoptic gospels, the high priest takes Jesus' response as a sign that he is guilty of blasphemy. In Matthew and Mark – essentially the same at this point – he tears his clothes, a powerful symbol of having heard a blasphemous statement. There's just one problem. According to Jewish law (specifically, a book in the Mishnah known as Sanhedrin 7.5), the only way one can commit blasphemy is to speak the divine name of God, and Jesus has not done that. Furthermore, if Jesus *did* pronounce such a statement in the hearing of the high priests, they would become witnesses to it, and the law was clear that you cannot act as a judge in a case where you are a witness. In other words, they are clutching at straws.

Comparing Matthew 26:57-68, Luke 22:54, 63-71

In Matthew's account (Matthew 26:57–68), which follows Mark very closely, the priests actually seek "false" testimony in order to put Jesus to death. Also, in verse 64, Jesus responds to the high priest's accusation with "you said it" instead of by saying "I am."

In Luke's account (Luke 22:54, 63–71), Jesus' answer to the high priest is more cryptic and yet, somehow, more honest. "If I tell you, you won't believe, and if I ask you a question, you won't answer." When pushed a little later on, Jesus simply says "you say that I am," which may be a way of pointing out that they're going to find him guilty no matter what; sometimes when we confront dishonest authority, it can be powerful to simply acknowledge its dishonesty.

In 2017, defending information given by then White House press secretary Sean Spicer, Kellyanne Conway, counsellor to the president, said that Spicer used "alternative facts." While it was quickly and widely pointed out that "alternative facts" are simply false statements, the idea stuck for many people. In this era of "alternative facts" and "fake news," the accusations against Jesus become a little more chilling.
■ How does it feel, to see Jesus being accused on trumped up, nonsense charges?
■ What does it say about the authorities who are presiding in this trial?

John 18:12b–24

[12b]They bound him [13]and led him first to Annas. He was the father-in-law of Caiaphas, the high priest that year. ([14]Caiaphas was the one who had advised the Jewish leaders that it was better for one person to die for the people.)

[15]Simon Peter and another disciple followed Jesus. Because this other disciple was known to the high priest,

he went with Jesus into the high priest's courtyard. ¹⁶However, Peter stood outside near the gate. Then the other disciple (the one known to the high priest) came out and spoke to the woman stationed at the gate, and she brought Peter in. ¹⁷The servant woman stationed at the gate asked Peter, "Aren't you one of this man's disciples?"

"I'm not," he replied. ¹⁸The servants and the guards had made a fire because it was cold. They were standing around it, warming themselves. Peter joined them there, standing by the fire and warming himself.

¹⁹Meanwhile, the chief priest questioned Jesus about his disciples and his teaching. ²⁰Jesus answered, "I've spoken openly to the world. I've always taught in synagogues and in the temple, where all the Jews gather. I've said nothing in private. ²¹Why ask me? Ask those who heard what I told them. They know what I said."

²²After Jesus spoke, one of the guards standing there slapped Jesus in the face. "Is that how you would answer the high priest?" he asked.

²³Jesus replied, "If I speak wrongly, testify about what was wrong. But if I speak correctly, why do you strike me?"²⁴Then Annas sent him, bound, to Caiaphas the high priest.

John 18:19–24 John does not contain a trial before Caiaphas, but instead offers us a snippet of conversation between Jesus and Annas. It is not at all impossible that this occurred, prior to Jesus being brought to Caiaphas (something John says occurred in verse 24). In this conversation, Jesus is clearly the "winner." We are not given Annas' answer, but I think he probably gulped a few times, and sent Jesus away.

Mark 14:66–72

⁶⁶Meanwhile, Peter was below in the courtyard. A woman, one of the high priest's servants, approached ⁶⁷and saw

Peter warming himself by the fire. She stared at him and said, "You were also with the Nazarene, Jesus."

⁶⁸But he denied it, saying, "I don't know what you're talking about. I don't understand what you're saying." And he went outside into the outer courtyard. A rooster crowed.

⁶⁹The female servant saw him and began a second time to say to those standing around, "This man is one of them." ⁷⁰But he denied it again.

A short time later, those standing around again said to Peter, "You must be one of them, because you are also a Galilean."

⁷¹But he cursed and swore, "I don't know this man you're talking about." ⁷²At that very moment, a rooster crowed a second time. Peter remembered what Jesus told him, "Before a rooster crows twice, you will deny me three times." And he broke down, sobbing.

This is a very well-known and well-illustrated part of the passion story. It appears in all four gospels and is one of the stories we can perhaps most easily insert ourselves into. Can we not all readily imagine ourselves, backed into a corner, offering what seems to be a small, dishonest statement to protect ourselves without thinking through the consequences? The consequences are intriguing here, because this incident does not really advance the overall story. In other words, it is not as if anything happens to Jesus as a result of Peter's denial, other than the fact that Jesus clearly feels additionally abandoned.

■ Think about those times when you have denied your faith. What has led you to hide your Christian faith?
■ How do you feel when you do that?

Mark 14:70 The mention of Peter being Galilean is a small clue that attests to the story's authenticity. Why make up a point like that? Since all three synoptic gospels include it, it's possible this story happened pretty much the way it is presented to us. However, it's also worth noting that a number of scholars in the middle of the last century questioned the story in its entirety, suggesting that it had been invented to put Peter in a less than favourable light. This is certainly possible, although doubtful. If Peter were being put down to elevate someone else – such as Mary Magdalene, the first apostle of the risen Christ – it would make sense to emphasize that individual in the story, at Peter's expense, but that does not happen. Of course, this could simply be because Mary is a woman.

> There is an extra sting in this story, for Peter has been a leader among the disciples and is one of Jesus' closest friends and followers.
> ■ What might it tell us that even Peter cannot be faithful to Jesus all the time?
> ■ What might that say about our own faith journey?

Earlier, Jesus had told Peter that he would deny knowing Jesus that very night, which leads to the mention of a rooster crowing. The significance is not the rooster, nor the number of times it crows (which is good, because the gospels are not consistent here). Rather, the significance is that Peter will deny Jesus three times that very night, before morning.

Comparing Matthew 26:69–75, Luke 22:56–62, John 18:25–27

Once again, Matthew's account follows Mark very closely, with a few small differences. In Matthew 26:73, rather than tell us that Peter is Galilean, Matthew has an accuser notice his Galilean accent. Also, Peter's response at the end of the story (verse 75) is magnified: Matthew tells us he sobbed "uncontrollably."

In Luke 22:56, rather than accuse Peter directly, a woman first tells others that Peter was with Jesus.

Luke's account (Luke 22:56–62) also provides an additional element. Prior to this, Luke has tried to avoid anything that would shame the disciples, yet here Jesus turns and stares at Peter, which leads to Peter's "uncontrollable" tears.

In John's account (John 18:25–27), the first of Peter's denials (John 18:17) happens in the courtyard of the high priest before Jesus is questioned – in other words, before the two that appear in verses 25–27.

Closing Thoughts

It can be tempting to divinize Jesus in this story, to see him as superhuman, perhaps because Jesus appears to know beforehand that Peter will deny him. This is sometimes expanded to imply that Jesus had some kind of special knowledge of things, and could predict the future.

I would argue that the gospels do not suggest this at all. Rather, I believe they show us a Jesus who is incredibly human, who is raw and hurting and quite probably scared. Thus, it is an extreme blow when Peter, his best friend and the one who had promised to stick with him no matter what, squirms and says, "Nope, never met the guy."

At the same time, to be fair to Peter, we can surely understand *his* fear in all of this. In speaking of Peter's denial and subsequent sense of remorse, someone remarked, "this act of blatant sin and forgiveness gives me hope."

■ How do you respond emotionally to Peter's denial?

Interrogation and Condemnation

After reading a brief story about Judas in Matthew's gospel we shift to the interrogation by Pilate, on behalf of the Roman authorities. Notice that after his questioning of Jesus, Pilate comes to the conclusion that Jesus has done nothing wrong and chooses to set Jesus free. Even though he represents Rome and the power of Rome, Pilate appears to be intimidated by the people he governs; he wants to appease the religious leadership and, more importantly, is intimidated by the crowd, ultimately making his decision based on their repeated shouting, but not on his own conviction. Alternatively, Pilate is a very shrewd and sly political representative of Rome, as Roman politicians had to be. By saying he finds no fault with Jesus, he gets the Jews to condemn their own man, so to speak. In other words, in the future, he gets to say, "Hey, don't blame Rome! *You're* the ones who wanted him gone!" It's a common oppressor tactic to get the people to fight among themselves. This is akin to how European countries manipulated the Blacks in colonial Africa, for example, setting tribes against each other, and creating false divisions.

Matthew 27:3–10

3When Judas, who betrayed Jesus, saw that Jesus was condemned to die, he felt deep regret. He returned the thirty pieces of silver to the chief priests and elders, and 4said, "I did wrong because I betrayed an innocent man."

But they said, "What is that to us? That's your problem." 5Judas threw the silver pieces into the temple and left. Then he went and hanged himself.

^{6}The chief priests picked up the silver pieces and said, "According to the Law it's not right to put this money in the treasury. Since it was used to pay for someone's life, it's unclean."^{7}So they decided to use it to buy the potter's field where strangers could be buried. ^{8}That's why that field is called "Field of Blood" to this very day. ^{9}This fulfilled the words of Jeremiah the prophet: And I took the thirty pieces of silver, the price for the one whose price had been set by some of the Israelites, ^{10}and I gave them for the potter's field, as the Lord commanded me.

This brief snippet is unique to Matthew; Luke includes a different story about the death of Judas, which appears in the book of Acts. Yet the story is believable, and may have been left out of the other gospels because they wanted no part in showing that Judas had a conscience.

When Judas realizes where things are going, he is overcome with guilt, suggesting that he did not want Jesus to be killed, but had other motivations. What were they? We can only speculate.

■ **Why do you think Judas turned Jesus in to the authorities?**

Matthew 27:6 The religious leaders do not want blood, or blood money, on their hands (or on their conscience), so they decide to donate it for the purchase of a field to be used as a cemetery for people without families who would otherwise take care of their burial.

Mark 15:1–5

At daybreak, the chief priests – with the elders, legal experts, and the whole Sanhedrin – formed a plan. They bound Jesus, led him away, and turned him over to Pilate.

^{2}Pilate questioned him, "Are you the king of the Jews?"

Jesus replied, "That's what you say." [3]*The chief priests
were accusing him of many things.*

[4]*Pilate asked him again, "Aren't you going to answer?
What about all these accusations?"* [5]*But Jesus gave no
more answers, so that Pilate marveled.*

This is often referred to as the "trial before Pilate," or the
"political trial," so it is vital right off the bat to note that
it is *not* a trial – at least not in any way that we would
understand a trial today. This story is about accusation
and persecution, leading to crowd control and mob in-
fluence, culminating in death. There is no real legal sense
to it at all.

Hanging over the entire story of the death of Jesus is
the issue of who was responsible. Tradition has sought
either to paint the Roman government as the "bad guys,"
or the Jews. The latter interpretation has had horrific ef-
fects for the Jewish people; Christians have a long history of persecuting the Jews as "Christ killers." We must
be incredibly careful, therefore, to remember that the issue here is of persecution *within* a religion. Jesus was
Jewish. There were no "Christians" during Jesus' day, and
obviously no such thing as Christianity. Jesus, a Jew, challenged the Jewish religious *authorities*, trying to bring
his faith community back to its roots of justice and fair-
ness, and they are the ones who killed him.

A more modern equivalent to what happened to Jesus
can be found in the famous "red scare" that swept through
the United States in the 1950s. Some Americans accused
other Americans of being Communists, persecuting them
and destroying their careers. This was not an "anti-Ameri-
can" thing coming from outside the country, but a home-
grown, domestic, systematic process designed by some
of those in power to get rid of "undesirables." Jesus is an
undesirable, for he dared to confront the authorities at
every turn, and for that will pay the price of death.

Mark 15:2 Pilate asks a simple question: "Are you the king of the Jews?" This question might give Pilate some room to maneuver, because it could potentially show Jesus as a threat to the power of Rome. But Jesus' refusal to own the accusation – his retort, "That's what you say," doesn't really answer it at all – leaves Pilate not knowing what to do.

Comparing Matthew 27:1–2, 11–14; Luke 23:1–5; John 18:28–38

Matthew's account is very similar to Mark's story. Pilate makes an accusation and Jesus simply says, "That's what you say."

■ Why do you think Jesus does not answer Pilate's question directly?
■ Why do you think Pilate marvelled, or was amazed, at Jesus' answer?

Luke's account (Luke 23:1–5) shifts the story a little. The assembly of religious leaders is involved in making accusations against Jesus, and they up the ante by saying that he oppose the payment of taxes to Caesar, hoping to appeal to Pilate's sense of loyalty to Rome. Pilate, after his brief interrogation, declares "I find no legal basis for action against this man" (Luke 23:4–5). This is a reminder that the case against Jesus really isn't about law anyway, but about those in power feeling threatened, and wanting to rid themselves of this problem. This is further emphasized by their statement that Jesus "agitates the people with his teaching."

John 18:28–38

28 The Jewish leaders led Jesus from Caiaphas to the Roman governor's palace. It was early in the morning. So that they could eat the Passover, the Jewish leaders

 STUDY

**Death of
Jesus**
FOR
Progressive
Christians

wouldn't enter the palace; entering the palace would have made them ritually impure. ²⁹So Pilate went out to them and asked, "What charge do you bring against this man?"

³⁰They answered, "If he had done nothing wrong, we wouldn't have handed him over to you."

³¹Pilate responded, "Take him yourselves and judge him according to your Law."
The Jewish leaders replied, "The Law doesn't allow us to kill anyone." (³²This was so that Jesus' word might be fulfilled when he indicated how he was going to die.)

³³Pilate went back into the palace. He summoned Jesus and asked, "Are you the king of the Jews?"

³⁴Jesus answered, "Do you say this on your own or have others spoken to you about me?"

³⁵Pilate responded, "I'm not a Jew, am I? Your nation and its chief priests handed you over to me. What have you done?"

³⁶Jesus replied, "My kingdom doesn't originate from this world. If it did, my guards would fight so that I wouldn't have been arrested by the Jewish leaders. My kingdom isn't from here."

³⁷"So you are a king?" Pilate said.
Jesus answered, "You say that I am a king. I was born and came into the world for this reason: to testify to the truth. Whoever accepts the truth listens to my voice."

³⁸"What is truth?" Pilate asked.
After Pilate said this, he returned to the Jewish leaders and said, "I find no grounds for any charge against him."

In typical fashion, John's story (John 18:28–38) is different. Unlike the other gospels, he presents us with a lengthier version of the interrogation by Pilate.

John 18:28 There is much in this simple statement about the Jewish leadership not wanting to defile themselves. It was considered unlawful to visit anyone from another nation, and thus to enter Pilate's palace would have rendered them ritually unclean. One might applaud them for wanting to maintain their purity, yet a short time later (John 19:15) they will sell out their own faith claiming loudly that "we have no king but Caesar." Clearly, John wants us to note the hypocrisy of the religious leadership.

A larger question occurs, though, in the fact that the Passover meal would have been eaten the night before (Thursday), and thus we are out of sync on dates. Because John wants Jesus sacrificed at the same time as the Passover lambs, because this symbolism is important, the Passover meal must occur *after* the death of Jesus. Thus, in John's gospel, either the dating is "wrong," or John has Jesus crucified on Thursday rather than Friday.

■ **What is your own experience of religious hypocrisy?**

John 18:29–31 Pilate's conversation with the religious leaders differs from the other gospels. First, rather than make an accusation, the leadership rather haughtily says "if Jesus hadn't done anything wrong we wouldn't have brought him here." Pilate's response of "judge him yourselves" yields the intriguing statement that "the law doesn't allow us to kill anyone." Except that wasn't true.

If Jesus is guilty of blasphemy, then the religious leaders have every right to kill him – it's a capital offence, and there is biblical precedent. However, they seem to want to pass off the responsibility. This adds to the sense of their hypocrisy: "*We* have found him guilty, but *we* don't want to be held accountable for doing anything about it."

Jesus and Pilate then go on to have a conversation about whether Jesus is the Jewish king or not. Imagine

An unbelieved truth can hurt a man much more than a lie. It takes great courage to back truth unacceptable to our times. There's a punishment for it, and it's usually crucifixion.
– John Steinbeck, *East of Eden*

the scene: Pilate dressed in the garb of Roman authority; Jesus grubby, wearing a gown that probably shows far too much wear and tear. It's almost laughable that Pilate would ask Jesus if he were a king! It seems Pilate is trying to get behind the accusation and sincerely wants to know who Jesus is. The conversation ends with Pilate declaring that he can find no charge to bring against Jesus.

> Theologian Tom Long understands Jesus' statement "you say so" as being akin to "Yes, I am King of the Jews, but I do not accept your definitions of kingship, and I do not need your permission."
> ■ What do you think of this rendition of Jesus' words?
> ■ What other meaning might his answer have?

Luke 23:6–16

⁶Hearing this, Pilate asked if the man was a Galilean. ⁷When he learned that Jesus was from Herod's district, Pilate sent him to Herod, who was also in Jerusalem at that time. ⁸Herod was very glad to see Jesus, for he had heard about Jesus and had wanted to see him for quite some time. He was hoping to see Jesus perform some sign. ⁹Herod questioned Jesus at length, but Jesus didn't respond to him. ¹⁰The chief priests and the legal experts were there, fiercely accusing Jesus. ¹¹Herod and his soldiers treated Jesus with contempt. Herod mocked him by dressing Jesus in elegant clothes and sent him back to Pilate. ¹²Pilate and Herod became friends with each other that day. Before this, they had been enemies.

¹³Then Pilate called together the chief priests, the rulers, and the people. ¹⁴He said to them, "You brought this man before me as one who was misleading the people. I have questioned him in your presence and found nothing in this man's conduct that provides a legal basis for the charges you have brought against him. ¹⁵Neither

did Herod, because Herod returned him to us. He's done nothing that deserves death. [16]Therefore, I'll have him whipped, then let him go."

Unique to Luke, this story indicates that Pilate wants to pass the buck to someone else – in this case, Herod the king of Galilee. This may well be a clever strategic move on Pilate's part, to have Jesus sentenced by the ostensible Jewish ruler. This is not the Herod of the time of Jesus' birth, but one of his sons. He was a tyrant. We are told that Herod was anxious to meet Jesus, hoping to see him perform some signs, and he questions Jesus at length. When Jesus does not respond, Herod's anger grows. Pilate and Herod now become friends.

Luke 23:13–16 All this leads Pilate to say to the religious leaders that he has thoroughly questioned Jesus, and finds nothing wrong with him, and Herod has found nothing either. He rather blandly says, "I'll just have him whipped and let him go."

■ As the story unfolds, who do you feel is responsible for the death of Jesus?

Mark 15:6–14

[6]During the festival, Pilate released one prisoner to them, whomever they requested. [7]A man named Barabbas was locked up with the rebels who had committed murder during an uprising. [8]The crowd pushed forward and asked Pilate to release someone, as he regularly did. [9]Pilate answered them, "Do you want me to release to you the king of the Jews?" [10]He knew that the chief priests had handed him over because of jealousy. [11]But the chief priests stirred up the crowd to have him release Barabbas to them instead. [12]Pilate replied, "Then what do you want me to do with the one you call king of the Jews?"

¹³They shouted back, "Crucify him!"

¹⁴Pilate said to them, "Why? What wrong has he done?"

They shouted even louder, "Crucify him!"

In the 2016 U.S. presidential election campaign, then-candidate Donald Trump sought to make a major issue out of the "illegal" email activity of his opponent, Hillary Clinton, to steer people away from some of the accusations of his own illegal activity. At Trump rallies, the crowd would be whipped into a frenzy, chanting "Lock her up!" in response to almost anything. The sense for many was that Clinton's days were numbered and that a legal trial would occur within minutes of Trump's inauguration. However, few were surprised when the issue was dropped as soon as Trump was elected president. Interestingly, when asked about the Clinton's illegal behaviour, few Trump supporters understood any of the issues – but they wanted her locked up. A similar thing occurs at this point in Jesus' story. The crowd is whipped into a frenzy, probably without really knowing what is going on or why.

Mark 15:6 The crowd remind Pilate that, by tradition, he is to release a prisoner, There appear to be only two under consideration: Jesus and Barabbas, who was locked up with the rebels who had committed murder during an uprising.

Mark 15:12–14 When Pilate asks the first time what the crowd wants done with Jesus, they shout "crucify him!" When he pushes the issue and asks "Why?" they do not respond, but simply shout all the louder "crucify him!" The point seems clear: the reasons don't matter, they just want Jesus dead.

Comparing Matthew 27:15–23; Luke 23:17–23; John 18:39–40, 19:1–15

Curiously, in Matthew's account (Matthew 27:15–23) the gospel writer expands the name of Barabbas, adding the first name "Jesus." While no other gospel names Barabbas this way, rendering Matthew's version a bit suspect, there is a delightful irony that Jesus Barabbas literally means "Jesus, son of the father" in Aramaic.

Unique to Matthew, Matthew 27:19 appears to be a part of Matthew's scheme to show Pilate in a rather positive light, and by extension show that it was the religious leadership that was the problem. Pilate's wife sends a message in which she declares Jesus to be righteous (innocent). This positive image of Pilate may be explained by the fact that Matthew is writing for a church that is likely half Jewish and half Gentile, thus he tends to paint both groups in equal ways. His version of the story suggests that it is the religious leadership who are the problem – and who were still a problem in the early church, when the gospel was written.

In Luke's account (Luke 23:17–23), there is no conversation about the custom of releasing a prisoner, although the assumption that Pilate will do it is clearly present. What is more unique to Luke, however, is the statement that Pilate wanted to release Jesus, although the crowd shouts him down. This lets us know that Pilate considered the "evidence" against Jesus to be very flimsy, and also that Pilate was afraid of the crowd. Or it tells us that Pilate had achieved his strategic goal and got the crowd to pass sentence.

Once again, John's account (John 18:39–40, 19:1–15) is a much longer version of essentially the same story, with many details added. In John 19:2–5, the soldiers dress Jesus in mock finery. Pilate brings Jesus out dressed in the mock robe and crown of thorns, after he has been beaten, and asks the crowd if they *really* think he is a

threat. The response to this – "Crucify!" comes only from the religious leaders. In John 19:8, the gospel writer makes a point of saying that Pilate is scared. The story comes to a climax in verse 15, when Pilate says, "you really want me to kill your king?" and they shout back "we have no king but Caesar." This veritable pledge of allegiance to a foreign and oppressive ruler is tantamount to blasphemy, and thus in an instant condemns the religious leadership.

Mark 15:15

¹⁵*Pilate wanted to satisfy the crowd, so he released Barabbas to them. He had Jesus whipped, then handed him over to be crucified.*

Jesus is now given up to be killed. Pilate, representing all the power in the Mediterranean world at the time, gives in to the crowd.

Comparing Matthew 27:24–26, Luke 23:24–25, John 19:16

Matthew's account (Matthew 27:24–26) expands Mark's presentation by adding the scene of Pilate washing his hands. On one level he is simply excusing himself from any guilt or responsibility for Jesus' death. However, on another level, he can also be seen as fulfilling the Jewish law, which stated that if a murdered body was found, the leaders of a community should wash their hands, proclaiming that they are innocent of the person's death. Thus – as is the case with the visit of the magi in Matthew 2 – Gentiles do for Jesus what Jews appear not to do.

The statement "let his blood be on us and on our children" (Matthew 27:25) has led to much misunderstanding and inter-religious hatred over the centuries, but that is not at all what Matthew intended. Matthew wants us to know that there are good Jews and good Gentiles in this story – it is only the ones who take on the responsibility who are to be held accountable.

Luke's reading (Luke 23:24–25) is essentially the same as Mark's.

John 19:16 basically says the same as Mark and Luke, although he adds that the soldiers took Jesus prisoner. Perhaps he wants to show us that Pilate gives Jesus over, but not to the Jewish people – he is still in Roman custody, as he will remain until the end.

Mark 15:16–21

[16]*The soldiers led Jesus away into the courtyard of the palace known as the governor's headquarters, and they called together the whole company of soldiers.* [17]*They dressed him up in a purple robe and twisted together a crown of thorns and put it on him.* [18]*They saluted him, "Hey! King of the Jews!"* [19]*Again and again, they struck his head with a stick. They spit on him and knelt before him to honor him.* [20]*When they finished mocking him, they stripped him of the purple robe and put his own clothes back on him. Then they led him out to crucify him.*

[21]*Simon, a man from Cyrene, Alexander and Rufus' father, was coming in from the countryside. They forced him to carry his cross.*

Mark 15:16 The soldiers take Jesus inside, out of sight of the crowd, to torture and abuse him. It is a reminder to us that this is often how those in power treat those they deem as being beneath them (think of the U.S. government and the treatment of prisoners at Guantanamo Bay, for example).

Mark 15:17 They dress Jesus in a purple robe and crown of thorns. A purple robe, the colour of royalty, would have been well out of reach of the salaries of a group of soldiers, so this suggests they have borrowed it from Pilate.

> Christmas and Easter can be subjects for poetry, but Good Friday, like Auschwitz, cannot. The reality is so horrible it is not surprising that people should have found it a stumbling block to faith.
> – W. H. Auden, *A Certain World: A Commonplace Book*

Mark 15:18 "hail, King of the Jews" This is too similar to the traditional greeting given Caesar to be seen as anything but irony.

Mark 15:21 Simon of Cyrene (and his sons) We do not meet Simon (or his sons, who are mentioned only in Mark) anywhere else in the gospels, but here he is pressed into service to carry Jesus' cross. Why? It's a mystery, because the Romans always forced prisoners to carry their own cross – that is, the cross beam, to which their wrists would probably already be bound. This was an enormous weight, and very uncomfortable, making walking all the more difficult. The best explanation tradition has come up with – and there is nothing to say it couldn't have happened this way – is that Jesus had been flogged so severely he was too weak to carry his own cross. This would have been similar to what still happens today, where the state keeps prisoners on death row in good health up until the moment when it kills them; the Romans did not want to risk Jesus dying before he got to the place of execution. This explanation would be borne out by the fact that Jesus died quite quickly.

The naming of Alexander and Rufus suggests they (along with their father) had become members of the Christian community, and that their names were well-known by the readers of the gospel. It is also intriguing that their names are not Jewish, suggesting that the family was originally Gentile.

Comparing Matthew 27:27–32, Luke 23:26–32

In Matthew's account (Matthew 27:28–29), the soldiers dress Jesus in a "red military coat" and give him a stick to hold, another bit of mockery, as normally a king would hold a staff of some sort symbolizing power, not a stick that would break as soon as you tried to swing it. The "red military coat" is quite possibly Matthew's correction, since a purple cloak would have been difficult to acquire. Also, "military coat" conveys a bigger difference in English than is present in the original; Matthew simply wants us to understand that it is a garment that happened to be lying around.

Luke 23:26–32

[26]As they led Jesus away, they grabbed Simon, a man from Cyrene, who was coming in from the countryside. They put the cross on his back and made him carry it behind Jesus. [27]A huge crowd of people followed Jesus, including women, who were mourning and wailing for him. [28]Jesus turned to the women and said, "Daughters of Jerusalem, don't cry for me. Rather, cry for yourselves and your children. [29]The time will come when they will say, 'Happy are those who are unable to become pregnant, the wombs that never gave birth, and the breasts that never nursed a child.' [30]Then they will say to the mountains, 'Fall on us,' and to the hills, 'Cover us.' [31]If they do these things when the tree is green, what will happen when it is dry?"

[32]They also led two other criminals to be executed with Jesus.

Immediately we notice that Luke does not include an account of the mocking of Jesus. The reason for Mark including it is clear: his community is being persecuted and he wants to show that Jesus suffered the same persecution. No doubt Matthew included it because he was copying Mark. So the question becomes, why would Luke leave it out? Luke mentioned Jesus being dressed in finery when he was sent by Herod back to Pilate, so he may simply have thought that the story occurred there. Or he may simply want to reserve the expression of contempt for Jesus until after the crucifixion. (One early manuscript

of Luke has the crown of thorns being placed on Jesus' head when he is on the cross, suggesting that someone thought that part of the story belonged in Luke.)

Luke 23:28–31 Again, Luke inserts a piece that is missing from the other gospels. On the way to crucifixion, Jesus turns to a group of women and suggests they cry for themselves rather than for him. It carries a stark warning: a time will come when those who have no future – a barren womb – are better off. Jesus closes the pronouncement with a quotation: "if they do these things when the tree is green, what will happen when it is dry?" Some scholars believe this comes from a saying in the Midrash, in response to bad things happening to good people: "If this can happen to those who do the will of God, what will happen to those who do *not* do God's will?" In other words, Jesus may be saying, "Look, if they're going to do this to me – someone who was fairly well known, with a following – for proclaiming God's love and justice, can you imagine what will happen to ordinary, everyday folk?"

Luke 23:32 The mention of the criminals is written in a very convoluted form in the Greek manuscripts, suggesting that the writer took great pains to list these people as criminals, but wanted to make sure the reader did not understand that Jesus was also a criminal.

John 19:17

[17]Carrying his cross by himself, he went out to a place called Skull Place (in Aramaic, Golgotha).

John 19:17 "Carrying his cross by himself ..." This piece is typical John – he reinforces his theology that Jesus has lain down his life quite willingly, and that no one has forced him to do it. Thus, it makes sense that he would "carry his cross by himself."

None of the gospels tell us exactly where Jesus was killed. They all refer to a place called "Skull Hill" or "Skull Place" (*Golgotha* in Aramaic) but there is no agreement among scholars as to the location. Hebrews 13:12 and centuries of tradition tell us that it is outside the walls of the city of Jerusalem, which was the traditional venue for the crucifixion of blasphemers. It may have been the preferred place for the death of all criminals at Roman hands, as this blatant exertion of their power challenged Jewish sensibilities.

BIBLE STUDY

Death of Jesus
FOR
Progressive
Christians

The synoptic gospels and John offer two images. In the synoptics, Jesus is suffering greatly at this point in the story – to the point that he cannot carry his own cross. In John, he may be defiantly standing up to Rome and his own religious leadership by carrying his cross to his death.
■ What are the pros and cons of each image for you?
■ Which one makes the most sense to you?

Closing Thoughts

This may seem an odd place to stop, with Jesus on the way to the place of crucifixion, but it allows us to pause and contemplate all that has happened up to this point.

Was arriving at this point inevitable? Is there something that someone could have done – Peter, Judas, other disciples, even Jesus himself – that might have changed the outcome?

Beyond that, *should* the outcome have been changed? It is a hard question to consider, but we are left with the reality of the incredible importance of this story to our faith. That does not make the crucifixion necessary *then*, but it does make it necessary *now*.

■ What do we do with all these confused emotions as we approach the cross?

The crucifixion is the touchstone of Christian authenticity, the unique feature by which everything else, including the resurrection, is given its true significance.
– Fleming Rutledge, *The Crucifixion: Understanding the Death of Jesus*

Crucifixion and Burial

The interrogation is over, the sentence is pronounced, and Jesus has now arrived at the place of crucifixion. It has been coming for quite some time – you don't offend the religious and civil powers the way Jesus did and get away with it for long. So now we follow Jesus on this final leg of his journey.

As you read and explore these final moments of Jesus' life, try to imagine that you have not heard the story before, and that you do not know what will happen next.

Mark 15:22–26

22They brought Jesus to the place called Golgotha, which means Skull Place. 23They tried to give him wine mixed with myrrh, but he didn't take it. 24They crucified him. They divided up his clothes, drawing lots for them to determine who would take what. 25It was nine in the morning when they crucified him. 26The notice of the formal charge against him was written, "The king of the Jews."

Mark 15:23 Jesus is offered a narcotic mixture – essentially a painkiller – commonly given to those who were dying. Tradition has generally inserted an understanding that Jesus refused this because he chose to suffer – even wanted to suffer – and that he would rather drink the cup God had set before him. I don't want to say this is not true, but there is also the simple possibility that Jesus was at this point delirious. He has been beaten; he has probably had garbage tossed at him as he went down the road; he has been stripped naked in the hot sun, and nailed to a piece of wood. We know he is in such poor shape that he will die in a matter of hours rather than days, so it is not impossible that he didn't know what was going on. Yet another possibility that has been put forward is that Jesus thought it was poison. This may seem odd, given that he was in the process of dying, but the human will is strong, and the desire to survive, even when all seems to be lost, is incredibly strong.

For some, the suggestion that Jesus was *not* choosing to suffer but may have been simply delirious is difficult to accept, yet it provides the opportunity to explore a key aspect of the story: suffering.

■ How important is it for you that Jesus suffers in the story of his death?
■ Do you think he intentionally chose suffering whenever possible, or did it just turn out that way?

Mark 15:24 One was crucified naked, probably for the dual reason that it further humiliated the condemned, and also that this enabled someone (in Jesus' case at least, the soldiers) to keep the person's clothes. Artists have almost always added a loincloth, wanting to preserve a sense of dignity, and avoid offending viewers' eyes. But virtually all evidence points to the contrary.

Mark 15:25 nine in the morning This is not highly significant, except that none of the other gospel writers note it. Some have suggested that it corresponds to the 9 a.m. arrival of God's Spirit in the Pentecost story (Acts 2:1–21). However, given that Acts was written by a different author, this is a bit dubious.

Mark 15:26 All four gospels note that the crime for which Jesus was crucified – being "king of the Jews" – was written on a sign and placed on the cross. It is ironic that as he was dying, Jesus was labelled "king" – no won-

BIBLE STUDY

Death of Jesus
FOR
Progressive
Christians

der John adds some conversation about this point (see below).

Comparing Matthew 27:33–37, Luke 23:33–34

In Matthew's account (Matthew 27:33–37), Jesus at first tastes the wine and then refuses it, suggesting that he was quite aware of what he was doing. Some see here an affirmation that Jesus preferred to suffer, while others believe Jesus simply found it distasteful.

In Luke's account (Luke 23:33–34), no wine is offered, nor is the sign placed over Jesus' head; that will come later. In an amazing gesture, Jesus asks God to forgive those who killed him (Luke 23:34). This is in keeping with Luke's desire to portray Jesus' compassion. The significance of these words is discussed more fully in Appendix 3: The Seven Last Words (available as a free download, see page 92). However, it must be noted here that some ancient manuscripts of Luke's gospel do not have this phrase and this is, in turn, reflected in some (but not all) modern English translations, most notably the *New Revised Standard Version*. One has to wonder, then, if it was inserted so that when Stephen says something similar at his death (Acts 7:60) he is seen as quoting Jesus? Or is it in fact original, but somehow did not make it into the earliest manuscripts? We cannot know for sure.

John 19:18–27

18That's where they crucified him – and two others with him, one on each side and Jesus in the middle. 19Pilate had a public notice written and posted on the cross. It read "Jesus the Nazarene, the king of the Jews." 20Many of the Jews read this sign, for the place where Jesus was crucified was near the city and it was written in Aramaic, Latin, and Greek. 21Therefore, the Jewish chief priests complained to Pilate, "Don't write, 'The king of the Jews' but 'This man said, "I am the king of the Jews."'"

²²Pilate answered, "What I've written, I've written."

²³When the soldiers crucified Jesus, they took his clothes and his sandals, and divided them into four shares, one for each soldier. His shirt was seamless, woven as one piece from the top to the bottom. ²⁴They said to each other, "Let's not tear it. Let's cast lots to see who will get it." This was to fulfill the scripture,

They divided my clothes among themselves,
and they cast lots for my clothing.
That's what the soldiers did.

²⁵Jesus' mother and his mother's sister, Mary the wife of Clopas, and Mary Magdalene stood near the cross. ²⁶When Jesus saw his mother and the disciple whom he loved standing nearby, he said to his mother, "Woman, here is your son." ²⁷Then he said to the disciple, "Here is your mother." And from that time on, this disciple took her into his home.

John 19:19–22 Pilate has the sign about Jesus' crime written in Aramaic, Latin, and Greek – a symbolic suggestion that he wanted the world to know this. When some religious leaders complain, Pilate says curtly, "What I've written, I've written." Here again, John shows Pilate arguing with the religious leaders wanting to emphasize yet again that the death of Jesus was at their hands. And again we need to remember this is not a condemnation of their Jewishness, but rather of their inflexibility to reform their faith.

John 19:23–25 John's story about what happened to Jesus' clothing is generally understood as symbolism rather than fact. While all other gospels tell us that the soldiers divided Jesus' clothing by casting lots (seen as fulfilling Psalm 22:18), John goes a step further and speaks of a garment woven in one piece. This is not im-

"Ay," he said aloud. There is no translation for this word and perhaps it is just a noise such as a man might make, involuntarily, feeling the nail go through his hands and into the wood. – Ernest Hemingway, *The Old Man and the Sea*

possible – a fairly simple loom can produce a piece that needs no seams at the side – but the question would be "why?" John loves symbolism. Some believe the garment with no seams is meant to symbolize a garment that the high priest would wear, emphasizing this aspect of Jesus' ministry. Alternatively, some see it is a profound symbol of unity, and thus a preview of the need for unity within the church. These are, of course, only guesses.

John 19:25 All of the gospels will mention the presence of women at the cross in the closing hours of Jesus' life. This must not be overlooked, especially given that women are not often mentioned in the Bible. In defence of the male disciples who ran away, some argue that they were far more at risk than the women were. However, there is nothing to support this very strongly. Women who were seen as being on the "wrong" side of the government would have been just as likely to be punished as men. The women, however, stayed. Beyond that, it is women alone who are the first to encounter the story of the resurrection.

■ How do you understand the role of women in the story of the death of Jesus?
■ How do you understand the role of women in the entire story of Jesus' life?
■ Where does this leave the men?

John 19:26–27 Jesus sees his mother, and the "beloved disciple," and tells them they are now linked as mother and son. People have often sought to find here proof that Joseph has died previously (which may or may not have happened). They also note that Jesus' statement here would suggest that he has no other siblings, for if he did they would simply care for Mary. Thus, some see this as "proof" that Mary was a perpetual virgin.

Except that the text doesn't say that. We simply cannot know from what is presented here if Jesus' primary concern is for Mary, who would have been left as a nonperson if she had no male relative, or if it is for the disciple he had loved so dearly, who now finds himself without the close friend whom he had always looked up to and admired. Either way, this is a most compassionate act.

Mark 15:27–32

27 *They crucified two outlaws with him, one on his right and one on his left.*

29 *People walking by insulted him, shaking their heads and saying, "Ha! So you were going to destroy the temple and rebuild it in three days, were you?* 30 *Save yourself and come down from that cross!"*

31 *In the same way, the chief priests were making fun of him among themselves, together with the legal experts. "He saved others," they said, "but he can't save himself.* 32 *Let the Christ, the king of Israel, come down from the cross. Then we'll see and believe." Even those who had been crucified with Jesus insulted him.*

Mark 15:27 Others were crucified with Jesus, perhaps to remind us that this is something the Romans did frequently. One of the key reasons why they eventually moved away from crucifixion was that there were too many and it simply took too long.

Mark 15:28 Most translations do not include verse 28; it is assumed to be an addition. It simply quotes Isaiah 53:12, telling us "He was numbered among criminals." Since Mark seldom quotes Hebrew scriptures, it is assumed to be an addition.

Mark 15:29–32a The people passing by, including religious leaders, mock Jesus. The claim they point to, how-

---

ever, is not that Jesus is king of the Jews (despite the sign over his head) but rather his claim to rebuild the temple, the dwelling place of God. This may be the author's way of reminding us that people just didn't get what Jesus was talking about.

> ■ How do you feel when people do not "get" what another is saying?
> ■ How do you counter that?

Mark 15:32b Mark and Matthew both tell us that the criminals crucified with Jesus insulted him; Luke shows us a very different conversation.

Comparing Matthew 27:38–44

Matthew's version (Matthew 27:38–44) basically quotes Mark, simply fleshing out the story slightly, but not adding any significantly new information.

Luke 23:39–43

[39] *One of the criminals hanging next to Jesus insulted him: "Aren't you the Christ? Save yourself and us!"*

[40] *Responding, the other criminal spoke harshly to him, "Don't you fear God, seeing that you've also been sentenced to die?* [41] *We are rightly condemned, for we are receiving the appropriate sentence for what we did. But this man has done nothing wrong."* [42] *Then he said, "Jesus, remember me when you come into your kingdom."*

[43] *Jesus replied, "I assure you that today you will be with me in paradise."*

Luke's account (Luke 23:36) is similar to the ones in Mark and Matthew. Unlike Mark and Matthew, however, Luke has only one of the criminals insult Jesus. The second criminal rebukes the first, and points out that Jesus has been wrongly convicted. He then asks Jesus to remember him, and Jesus replies "today you will be with me in paradise." For more on this phrase, see The Seven Last Words (available as a free download, see page 92). Where did Luke get this story and how do we reconcile it with the other accounts? Because the other gospels don't include it, it seems likely that Luke may have added the story to emphasize again that Jesus is compassionate, even in the midst of his own suffering. Moments before his own death Jesus is still proclaiming God's message of forgiveness and unconditional love.

Mark 15:33–41

33From noon until three in the afternoon the whole earth was dark. 34At three, Jesus cried out with a loud shout, "Eloi, eloi, lama sabachthani," which means, "My God, my God, why have you left me?"

35After hearing him, some standing there said, "Look! He's calling Elijah!"

36Someone ran, filled a sponge with sour wine, and put it on a pole. He offered it to Jesus to drink, saying, "Let's see if Elijah will come to take him down." 37But Jesus let out a loud cry and died.

38The curtain of the sanctuary was torn in two from top to bottom. 39When the centurion, who stood facing Jesus, saw how he died, he said, "This man was certainly God's Son."

40Some women were watching from a distance, including Mary Magdalene and Mary the mother of James (the younger one) and Joses, and Salome. 41When Jesus was in Galilee, these women had followed and supported him, along with many other women who had come to Jerusalem with him.

Mark 15:33 Matthew and Luke parallel Mark's statement that darkness covered the earth from noon to three. This implies that the crucifixion took place at noon, al-

though Mark has said at 9 a.m. Ultimately, it doesn't matter. The consistent piece is that Jesus dies at 3 p.m.

Mark 15:34 Jesus cries out the first line of Psalm 22, a traditional lament with which most Jews would be familiar. What is intriguing, however, is that because it starts with the Hebrew *"Eli!"* (*"Eloi"* in Aramaic), which means "my God," some people thought Jesus was calling for Elijah to come and save him. Someone offers Jesus wine, again a narcotic to ease his suffering, but Jesus simply lets out a loud cry and dies. (For more on the expression see The Seven Last Words, available as a free download, see p. 92).

> Jesus' statement "My God, my God, why have you abandoned/ignored/forgotten/forsaken me?" – the word varies widely in English translation – is a challenge for some people, as it could be seen as showing Jesus in a moment of weakness. If he is the Son of God, and has known it for at least a major portion if not all of his life, why would he now appear to question it? However, taken literally, it is a profound statement of his faith. Some see in this a bold reminder that Jesus, while the Son of God, was also very human.
> ■ How does this cry of Jesus' sit with you?
> ■ What do you hear?

Mark 15:38 The sanctuary curtain prevented people from entering the holiest place in the temple (sometimes referred to as the Holy of Holies). When Jesus dies, the curtain is torn in two, signifying that God is now accessible. This veil separated God from the profane, but also shut God off from the people. In Mark's account, Jesus spoke of destroying the temple and raising it up again, which can be seen as taking place in this act of tearing, in that the temple sanctuary was now opened.

Mark 15:39 A Roman centurion, standing nearby, observes Jesus' death and declares that he was God's son – a way of noting that the centurion was indeed one of the chosen people, a true Jew. For those who questioned Jesus' faith to his religious heritage, this is a profound statement.

Mark 15:40–41 Here Mark mentions the women who were following Jesus, noting by name Mary Magdalene, James' and Joses' mother Mary, and Salome.

Comparing Matthew 27:45–56, Luke 23:44–49

Matthew's account (Matthew 27:45–56) follows Mark's story of the darkness covering the earth and the tearing of the temple curtain with a curious story of an earthquake, rocks being split, and people being raised from the dead (Matthew 27:51–53). In Matthew's birth narrative, creation also notices and responds with the great star that guided the magi. It is fitting, then, that some kind of similar phenomena occur at Jesus' death. Furthermore, it was believed that a key function of the Messiah was to raise the dead. Having this occur immediately upon the death of Jesus reinforces Matthew's point that Jesus was indeed the Messiah. It is a convenient – if convoluted – way of tidily closing off the life of Jesus.

In Luke's account (Luke 23:44–49) the tearing of the sanctuary curtain comes *before* the death of Jesus, almost as if it signals that his death is imminent.

Luke's version leaves out Jesus' quoting of Psalm 22, perhaps because Luke does not want to imply that Jesus was weak. However, he adds the phrase, "Father, into your hands I entrust my life." Jesus cries this in a loud voice, whereas in the other gospels Jesus simply cried out. The stories are not in conflict, but the shift in emphasis is curious. Luke also alters the centurion's comment (Luke 23:47), noting that Jesus was "righteous" rather than the Son of God. Finally, the people respond by beating their chests (Luke 23:48), a sign of mourning at the very least, and possibly a sign of contrition and recognition of their part in causing this to happen to Jesus.

John 19:28–30

28 After this, knowing that everything was already completed, in order to fulfill the scripture, Jesus said, "I am thirsty." 29 A jar full of sour wine was nearby, so the soldiers soaked a sponge in it, placed it on a hyssop branch, and held it up to his lips. 30 When he had received the sour wine, Jesus said, "It is completed." Bowing his head, he gave up his life.

As happens so many times, John's rendering of the account of the death of Jesus is quite different from the synoptic gospels. Jesus says different things, there is no mention of people's reaction, and the temple curtain does not tear.

John 19:28 "in order to fulfill the scriptures"
One might expect Matthew rather than John to say this. However, as is typical in John, the author wants to show that Jesus has total control of the situation.

The gospels writers present different accounts of and words at the moment of Jesus' death.
■ Does one or another story of this final act of Jesus' pre-resurrection life speak more clearly to you? Why?

John 19:29–30 Jesus is offered wine here, but only in response to what was essentially a request. After the wine, he declares, "It is completed," bows his head, and dies. Jesus dies in control and in prayer, not in agony.

Death of Jesus

FOR Progressive Christians

42 Since it was late in the afternoon on Preparation Day, just before the Sabbath, 43 Joseph from Arimathea dared to approach Pilate and ask for Jesus' body. (Joseph was a prominent council member who also eagerly anticipated the coming of God's kingdom.) 44 Pilate wondered if Jesus was already dead. He called the centurion and asked him whether Jesus had already died. 45 When he learned from the centurion that Jesus was dead, Pilate gave the dead body to Joseph. 46 He bought a linen cloth, took Jesus down from the cross, wrapped him in the cloth, and laid him in a tomb that had been carved out of rock. He rolled a stone against the entrance to the tomb. 47 Mary Magdalene and Mary the mother of Jesus saw where he was buried.

Mark 15:43 Here we meet Joseph of Arimathea. While later legends will portray him as Mary's great-uncle (or some other relative) and tell of him travelling to England (with or without Mary), there is nothing in scripture to support this. He plays a small but significant role in providing a tomb for Jesus. Mark tells us that he was a prominent member of the Sanhedrin, the Jewish council, who also awaited the coming of the realm of God. There is a possible conflict here, as Sanhedrin votes were anonymous, and had to be unanimous. Thus, had Joseph of Arimathea been present at the council meeting that decided Jesus' fate he must have voted in favour of condemnation. The easiest explanation is simply to surmise that Joseph was not present, although it is odd that he would be in Jerusalem when Jesus dies, but would not have been there a short time before, when the Sanhedrin voted to get rid of him. Some have suggested that Joseph did not know about the council meeting; it could make sense that they would not invite someone who might be favourable to Jesus.

> For me, the cross is an enactment of our human hatred. But what happens on Easter is the triumph of love in the midst of suffering. Isn't that reason for hope?
> – Serene Jones, president of Union Theological Seminary

Death of Jesus

FOR Progressive Christians

Comparing Matthew 27:57–61, Luke 23:50–56

Matthew's entire account (Matthew 27:57–61) is similar to Mark's, with only a few small but intriguing variations. First, Joseph is described as a "rich disciple of Jesus," which is not how Mark described him. Joseph's wealth is attested by the fact that he owns a stone tomb. The description of him as a disciple is particularly interesting, since it elevaties him up a notch from simply waiting eagerly for the realm of God. Matthew includes no mention that Joseph was a member of the Sanhedrin.

Luke's account (Luke 23:50–56) also follows both Mark and Matthew quite closely, giving credence to this part of the story. However, the author pointedly tells us that Joseph had not agreed with the plans of the Sanhedrin. Luke also adds a small note that the women watched where Jesus was buried so that they could prepare spices and bring them later to anoint Jesus' body. This sets things up for what will happen next in Luke's story.

John 19:31–42

³¹*It was the Preparation Day and the Jewish leaders didn't want the bodies to remain on the cross on the Sabbath, especially since that Sabbath was an important day. So they asked Pilate to have the legs of those crucified broken and the bodies taken down.* ³²*Therefore, the soldiers came and broke the legs of the two men who were crucified with Jesus.* ³³*When they came to Jesus, they saw that he was already dead so they didn't break his legs.* ³⁴*However, one of the soldiers pierced his side with a spear, and immediately blood and water came out.* ³⁵*The one who saw this has testified, and his testimony is true. He knows that he speaks the truth, and he has testified so that you also can believe.* ³⁶*These things happened to fulfill the scripture,* They won't break any of his bones. ³⁷*And*

another scripture says, They will look at him whom they have pierced.

[38]After this Joseph of Arimathea asked Pilate if he could take away the body of Jesus. Joseph was a disciple of Jesus, but a secret one because he feared the Jewish authorities. Pilate gave him permission, so he came and took the body away. [39]Nicodemus, the one who at first had come to Jesus at night, was there too. He brought a mixture of myrrh and aloe, nearly seventy-five pounds in all. [40]Following Jewish burial customs, they took Jesus' body and wrapped it, with the spices, in linen cloths. [41]There was a garden in the place where Jesus was crucified, and in the garden was a new tomb in which no one had ever been laid. [42]Because it was the Jewish Preparation Day and the tomb was nearby, they laid Jesus in it.

God is not found in the soul by adding anything but by a process of subtraction. – Meister Eckhart, 12th-century Christian mystic

John offers a rather detailed account (John 19:31–42) of what happened after Jesus died. The religious leaders want the bodies taken down from the crosses, and so Pilate authorizes the centurions to break the legs of the crucified men. While seemingly macabre, this was seen as a merciful act, as it hastened the death (essentially by suffocation) of those who had been nailed to a cross. When they come to Jesus, it is obvious that he has already died so the soldiers do not break his legs (to fulfill scripture), and instead pierce his side (again to fulfill scripture). The Greek verb *nyssein*, translated as "pierced," has more the sense of poking someone to wake them up; it was done to see if there might be a response from the crucified person, which contradicts the idea that the soldiers knew he was already dead. Obviously John is more interested in claiming that the scriptures were "fulfilled" than in anything else. We should not get sidetracked by what might have caused the flow of water and blood. Clearly John means it symbolically: the problem is that we have no satisfactory explanation of what sym-

bolism he was trying to invoke. Perhaps a best guess is that the blood represented that Jesus was indeed human; the water that he was living water, and thus God.

John 19:35 Some manuscripts omit this verse. It is a way for the author to emphasize that he has accurate sources for this information; think of it as a footnote or reference in a modern essay.

John 19:39 Here we see Nicodemus, the one who visited Jesus at night in John 3. It is to Nicodemus that Jesus said, "You must be born again." We also know that Nicodemus was a member of the Sanhedrin; what we do not know is whether he was present at the fateful meeting that condemned Jesus. If he was, he must have voted in favour because the vote had to be unanimous. This could explain the presentation of no less than 75 pounds of pure nard – perhaps it was a guilt offering. While some think this could be a scribal error, I would suggest that it probably is not. This massive amount fits well with John's desire to use exaggerated numbers to make a point, in this case to show that Nicodemus' present love for Jesus is so strong that he wants to provide a gargantuan, incomprehensible amount of ointment for his body. The point seems clear: Nicodemus had been filled with doubt (John 3), but now has come to realize that Jesus *is* the one chosen by God. Rather than a centurion, John uses Nicodemus to present this fact, in an extraordinary way.

Matthew 27:62–66

[62] *The next day, which was the day after Preparation Day, the chief priests and the Pharisees gathered before Pilate.* [63] *They said, "Sir, we remember that while that deceiver was still alive he said, 'After three days I will arise.'* [64] *Therefore, order the grave to be sealed until the third day. Otherwise, his disciples may come and steal the body*

and tell the people, 'He's been raised from the dead.' This last deception will be worse than the first."

⁶⁵Pilate replied, "You have soldiers for guard duty. Go and make it as secure as you know how." ⁶⁶Then they went and secured the tomb by sealing the stone and posting the guard.

Matthew offers this final footnote about the chief priests and Pharisees being concerned that Jesus' followers will steal the body, and then claim that he rose from the dead. Pilate sends soldiers for guard duty – a small, but significant, note that the tomb was well-guarded, and thus that the resurrection must have happened miraculously.

Final Thoughts

The story ends, kind of. For most Christians, of course, it doesn't really end because this story is meaningless without the continuation of Easter Sunday. Yet for the purposes of this study – and the purposes of history – there is a logical conclusion to these events. At this point, Jesus is dead and buried. As far as the world is concerned, the story is indeed over.

■ What feelings do you have as you contemplate this point in the journey?

■ Does this story in fact feel over and complete for you, or can you only hear it in the larger context of the resurrection at Easter?

1. Myth, Truth, and Fact

The stories about the life of Christ are best described as myth, but using that word can make some people of faith very nervous, because of the mistaken notion that the word myth means artificial. However, that is not inherently the case.

Merriam-Webster dictionary, on their website, offers this as a primary meaning of the word *myth:* "a usually traditional story of ostensibly historical events that serves to unfold part of the world view of a people or explain a practice, belief, or natural phenomenon." To put that another way, a myth is a story that may or may not be factual (more about that below) but that unfolds certain truths about a significant person, or helps to explain certain things. That tends to describe the stories about Jesus pretty well.

A further bit of definition from Merriam-Webster also says that a myth is "a popular belief or tradition that has grown up around something or someone." This is significant. The stories of Jesus are not well-corroborated outside of the Christian tradition, which can lead one to wonder about their historical accuracy. For many people of faith, especially in more conservative traditions, it seems vital to believe all the details about every story in the Bible, as if somehow the whole of "faith" might come crashing down if we were to introduce the element of doubt, even concerning tiny details. However, for many others, a broader, more open view can be not only helpful, but in fact freeing, and can contribute greatly to their own faith journey. As Finnish scholar Lauri Honko put it, "A myth expresses and confirms society's religious values and norms."

While certain stories are quite believable and appear in almost identical form in more than one gospel, there are also times when they differ – to the point that both cannot be factual. At other times, stories include elements that truly stretch the imagination a little too far. Did Jesus, for example, somehow make a few bread rolls and some fish multiply miraculously before people's eyes? Did he really walk on water? And what about all those healings, which take place in a variety of ways?

To understand the stories as myth can be very liberating, because it takes away the need to believe everything literally, and provides instead the opportunity to ask and explore how the stories can inform our lives. Let me give an example.

Many parts of the Bible challenge our logical minds. Other parts simply seem to contradict each other. We can try to pinch and squeeze and pretend certain details are not really there, in order to take all these things literally, or we can take them metaphorically, which I believe makes the stories stronger and more meaningful.

Read Mark 4:35–41. If we take this story literally, it has some intriguing benefit. For example, it tells us that should we happen to be in a boat on a lake, and Jesus is in the boat with us and a storm comes up, Jesus can stop the storm and the boat will not capsize. That's good news, but it's very limited.

On the other hand, if we take the story metaphorically, it tells us that when life becomes extremely difficult – as if we're in the midst of a storm, as if there is no hope and we're sinking – if we realize that Jesus is with us, we can probably get through it. For me, that carries a much stronger meaning and it has far more value for my day-to-day life. In other words, if we take the story metaphorically, it can apply to a far wider range of situations than if we take it literally, and it can have a stronger meaning for us. Such can be the power and value of myth.

Closely related to this is the distinction or tension between truth and fact. Many people equate the two, using them interchangeably. They understand a "true story" to be completely factual, yet such is not always the case.

Mark 4:35–41

[35]Later that day, when evening came, Jesus said to them, "Let's cross over to the other side of the lake." [36]They left the crowd and took him in the boat just as he was. Other boats followed along.

[37]Gale-force winds arose, and waves crashed against the boat so that the boat was swamped. [38]But Jesus was in the rear of the boat, sleeping on a pillow. They woke him up and said, "Teacher, don't you care that we're drowning?"

[39]He got up and gave orders to the wind, and he said to the lake, "Silence! Be still!" The wind settled down and there was a great calm. [40]Jesus asked them, "Why are you frightened? Don't you have faith yet?"

[41]Overcome with awe, they said to each other, "Who then is this? Even the wind and the sea obey him!"

Facts can be proven (or disproven) and are, by nature, true. However, there are truths that cannot be proven, yet they are still true. Here is an example from the Second World War.

Christian X was king of Denmark from 1912 to 1947. When Denmark was taken over by the Nazis, Christian refused to leave the country, and his defiance of the Nazis became legendary. It was well known that he would ride his horse through the streets of Copenhagen, unaccompanied by any guards, and this was a profound symbol for the Danish people of their ability to stand tall against the oppressor.

One day, a German soldier asked a Danish boy why the king rode without any guards, and he replied, "All of Denmark is his bodyguard." Another time, the Nazis attempted to fly their flag over the building being used as German army headquarters. The king told a German sentry that the flag must be removed. The sentry refused. The king then said, "I will send a soldier to take it down," and the sentry responded that the soldier would be shot. The king then declared, "That soldier will be me," and the flag was taken down.

The last – and probably most commonly repeated – story about King Christian concerns his decision, even though he wasn't Jewish, to wear a yellow star to show his solidarity with Danish Jews, who were required to wear a yellow Star of David. This in turn led many Danes to wear a yellow star, which stymied Nazis plans to differentiate the Jews and imprison them.

These are wonderful stories. They tell us much about King Christian and about the history of the Danish people. They are arguably all true stories, for there is a kernel of fact in each of them. They tell us about the Dane's defiance of the Nazis, and about their support for the Jewish people. Facts, however, are harder to find here.

For example, it is a well-known fact (in Denmark at least) that the king rode his horse, undefended, around Copenhagen, which greatly bolstered the Danish people in their defiance of the Nazis. The Nazi flag only flew for one day over German army headquarters so there is good reason to guess that *something* happened, but no one really knows what.

It is also well known that the king helped many Jews escape from Denmark. However, Danish Jews were never compelled to wear the yellow star, and no Dane ever wore one, let alone the king.

These stories are not "factual"; they were clearly invented. Yet one could readily argue that they are *true* stories, for the truth they carry is strongly embedded in them: the king *did* defy the Nazis, and this in turn inspired many Danes to follow suit. The king *did* help many Jews escape to neutral Sweden, and this ostensibly inspired many Danes to do the same, thus preventing almost all of Denmark's Jews from being captured and imprisoned and/or killed.

Truth and fact do *not* need to be the same thing. There is a statue of Abraham Lincoln located in Park Square in Boston. It shows Lincoln standing over an African slave, pardoning him. Did Lincoln actually do this? Technically, no. Yet he *did* do it on a much larger scale through his Emancipation Proclamation. Such are truth and fact. And such is the case with much of the Bible.

2. Why Did Jesus Die?

In exploring the biblical stories about the death of Jesus, it is good to ask the larger question hanging in the background of all this drama: Why did Jesus die?

Perhaps the most common understanding of the death of Jesus is what theologians refer to as "substitutionary atonement." Substitutionary atonement is based on the premise that we are all sinful and that God could rightly punish us with death. In Hebrew religious practice, of course, an animal was sacrificed instead, as a way of paying the price of the people's sin and restoring their relationship with God. According to Christian substitutionary atonement theology, the death of Jesus performs the same function as animal sacrifice. Jesus willingly dies, or is sacrificed by God, as a way to "pay" for our sins and restore our relationship with God.

Despite "atonement" theology being generally accepted by (too) many, there are some major flaws with this doctrine, besides its generally repugnant depiction of God.

First, it ignores the prophets. For centuries, God, speaking through prophets such as Isaiah, Hosea, and Amos, condemned the sacrificial cult as being a waste of time and even offensive to God. "I desire faithful love and not sacrifice," declares Hosea 6:6, "the knowledge of God instead of entirely burned offerings." It seems odd that, after having condemned the sacrificial cult for several hundred years, God would demand a sacrifice (in this case, nothing less than God's own son) on behalf of the people.

BIBLE STUDY

Death of Jesus
FOR
Progressive
Christians

> The pervasive idea of an abusive God-father who sends his own kid to the cross so God could forgive people is nuts.
> – Serene Jones, president of Union Theological Seminary

Second, this theology implies that God is bound by rules. Does God ever *have* to do anything? Of course not – if God is God. Thus, the idea that God would be bound by a rule – as if shrugging divine shoulders and saying, "Sorry, I wish someone didn't have to die, but my hands are tied" – presents us with an image of a rather "small" and ineffectual God. The Hebrew scriptures are filled with stories of God breaking rules, changing rules, and creating new rules out of great love and a desire for relationship with humankind. Would God suddenly reject all of that and hide behind a rule that *required* Jesus to die? It doesn't make sense.

In his book *Speaking Christian*, Marcus Borg points out that the idea of substitutionary atonement is a late development in theological history – its first appearance is in 1097, a thousand years after the writing of the Christian Bible. Borg points out that the meaning of Jesus' death becomes distorted if one assumes that it was necessary and required.

Contrary to atonement theory, scripture provides stronger responses to the question of why Jesus died. His message was revolutionary and a threat to the religious and political powers of the day. Talk of loving one's neighbours, of treating people as if they matter, of seeking forgiveness and new ways of being accountable to one another – these values do not encourage faithfulness to empire. Jesus' message was directly counter to the values that the government promoted. For them, there was no question but that Jesus had to be extinguished. To quote Marcus Borg, "The authorities said 'no' to Jesus but God said 'yes'" (*The Heart of Christianity*, p. 93).

Similarly the religious powers found their established order threatened as well. Jesus' theme of God's involvement in the world on behalf of the marginalized (specifically, foreigners, women, tax collectors, children, etc.) was a major challenge to the religious order of the day. It had to be stopped.

■ How do you understand the death of Jesus?
■ What explanations of it make sense to you?

3. The Seven Last Words

This is available as a download PDF on the Wood Lake website:
http://www.woodlake.com/djappendix3

Borg, Marcus. *The Heart of Christianity: Rediscovering a Life of Faith.* New York: HarperCollins, 2003.

— . *Speaking Christian: Why Words Have Lost Their Meaning and Power – and How They Can Be Restored.* New York: Harper Collins, 2011.

Borg, Marcus and John Dominic Crossan. *The Last Week: What the Gospels Really Teach about Jesus's Final Days in Jerusalem.* New York: HarperCollins, 2006.

Bromley, Geoffrey W. *Theological Dictionary of the New Testament – Abridged in One Volume.* Grand Rapids: Eerdmans, 1985.

Brown, Raymond E. *The Death of the Messiah – from Gethsemane to the Grave.* (Two volumes). New Haven: Yale University, 1994.

— . *The Gospel of John.* Garden City, NY: Doubleday, 1970.

Craddock, Fred B. *Luke: A Bible Commentary for Teaching and Preaching.* Louisville, KY: Westminster John Knox Press, 1990.

Hare, Douglas R. A. *Mark.* Louisville, KY: Westminster John Knox Press, 1996.

— . *Matthew: A Bible Commentary for Teaching and Preaching.* Louisville, KY: Westminster John Knox Press, 2009.

Henson, John H. *Good as New: a Radical Retelling of the Scriptures.* New York: O Books, 2004.

Honko, Lauri. *"The Problem of Defining Myth."* In Dundes, Alan (ed.). *Sacred Narrative: Readings in the Theory of Myth.* Oakland: University of California Press, 1988.

Long, Thomas G. *Matthew.* Louisville, KY: Westminster John Knox Press, 1997.

Malina, Bruce J. and Richard L. Rohrbaugh. *Social-Science Commentary on the Synoptic Gospels.* Minneapolis: Augsburg Fortress, 1992.

O'Day, Gail. R. and Susan E. Hylen. *John.* Louisville, KY: Westminster John Knox Press. 2006.

Sloyan, Gerard. *John: A Bible Commentary for Teaching and Preaching.* Louisville, KY: Westminster John Knox Press, 2009.

Williamson Jr., Lamar. *Mark: A Bible Commentary for Teaching and Preaching.* Louisville, KY: Westminster John Knox Press, 2009.

Birth of Jesus
for Progressive Christians

A FIVE SESSION STUDY GUIDE

Donald Schmidt

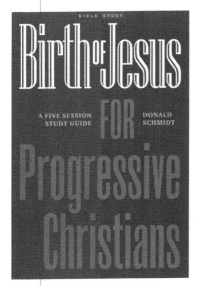

What if the Christmas story is not really what we think it is? What if things happened differently than tradition has maintained over the centuries? What if the biblical account differs – sometimes quite substantially – from the story most of us know from the nativity plays we participated in as children, or that our own children or grandchildren participate in? And what if the truth the authors of those stories are pointing to is not that Jesus was born in a miraculous way, but something that goes much deeper?

To some extent, each of us fashions our own version of the "Christmas story." Over time, as our associations and identification with that story grow, it can feel very uncomfortable and even disrespectful to disrupt or question that story. And yet these reactions can be instructive, for they beg larger questions about what's really important: the biblical narratives; or the traditions that have gathered around them, layered them, and at times obscured them; or the meaning all of this may have for our lives today?

ISBN 978-1-77343-287-8
5.5" x 8" | 80 pp | paperback | $14.95

Revelation
for Progressive Christians

A SEVEN SESSION STUDY GUIDE

Donald Schmidt

More material has probably been written about the biblical book of Revelation than the rest of the Bible combined – or at least it can seem that way. What's more, people who write or talk about Revelation often have a passion that defies all logic. They speak vividly and forcefully about plagues, and judgements, and the end of the world. All interesting themes – but are they the real concern or message of Revelation?

Revelation for Progressive Christians is a seven-session study guide that invites readers to explore Revelation as a fun, hope-filled book that contains a lot of fanciful imagery and symbolic references, to be sure, but that, at its core, offers words of assurance and hope to the church and its people today.

ISBN 978-1-77343-150-5
5.5" x 8" | 100 pp | paperback | $14.95

WOOD LAKE

Imagining, living, and telling the faith story.

WOOD LAKE IS THE FAITH STORY COMPANY.

It has told
■ the story of the seasons of the earth, the people of
God, and the place and purpose of faith in the world;
■ the story of the faith journey, from birth to death;
■ the story of Jesus and the churches that carry his
message.

Wood Lake has been telling stories for more than
35 years. During that time, it has given form and
substance to the words, songs, pictures, and ideas
of hundreds of storytellers.

Those stories have taken a multitude of forms –
parables, poems, drawings, prayers, epiphanies,
songs, books, paintings, hymns, curricula – all
driven by a common mission of serving those on
the faith journey.

Wood Lake Publishing Inc.

485 Beaver Lake Road
Kelowna, BC, Canada V4V 1S5
250.766.2778

www.woodlake.com